The Althouse Press
Faculty of Education, Western University
Porter, SURVIVING THE VALLEY TRAUMA AND BEYOND

SURVIVING THE VALLEY
TRAUMA AND BEYOND

Shirley Porter

THE ALTHOUSE PRESS
Geoffrey Milburn, Founding Director

First published in Canada in 2016 by
THE ALTHOUSE PRESS
Dean: *Vicki Schwean*
Director of Publications: *Gregory M. Dickinson*
Western Education, Western University, 1137 Western Road,
London, Ontario, Canada N6G 1G7

Copyright © 2016 by Western University, London, Ontario, Canada. No part of this publication may be reproduced, stored in a retrieval system, or transmitted in any form or by any means, electronic, photocopying, mechanical or otherwise, without the prior written permission of the publishers.

Illustrator, Editor: *Brian Bazett*
Cover Design: *Louise Gadbois*

Library and Archives Canada Cataloguing in Publication

Porter, Shirley, 1966-, author
    Surviving the valley : trauma and beyond / Shirley
    Porter.

ISBN 978-0-9950846-0-5 (paperback)

    1. Post-traumatic stress disorder--Treatment. 2. Psychic
    trauma--Treatment. I. Title.

RC552.P67P667 2015   616.85'2106   C2015-906666-2

www.traumaandbeyond.com

Designed, printed, and bound in Canada by Aylmer Express Limited, 390 Talbot Street East, Aylmer, Ontario.

This book is dedicated to those who find themselves in the valley of the shadow of death. You do not have to walk alone.

Table of Contents

Acknowledgments	xiii
Foreword	xv
Preface	xvii
An Introduction to the Valley	1

PART ONE: FIRST THINGS FIRST — 3

You Are Not Losing Your Mind	5
This Is Not about a Character Flaw	6
You Are a Survivor	7
The Journey to Healing	8
An Individual Journey	9
This Is BIG-Accept Help!	10
Finding a Therapist	11
Therapies That Work	12
Other Interventions That Might Help	14
What Can You Expect from Your Therapist?	15
If You Are Usually the Protector/Helper…	16
Being Strong Doesn't Mean You Aren't Exhausted	17
If You Are Suicidal…	18
Reflections	19

PART TWO: UNDERSTANDING TRAUMA — 21

What Is a Trauma? — 23
Post-Traumatic Stress Disorder (PTSD) — 25
Complex Post-Traumatic Stress Disorder — 26
Acute Stress Response — 27
Factors That Affect the Development of PTSD — 28
Protective Factors — 29
The Prevalence of Trauma — 30
The Scope of Trauma Response — 31
Reducing Distress Is the Priority — 32
Post-Trauma Responses — 33
Trauma and Your Body — 34
Trauma and Emotions — 35
Trauma and Thinking — 36
Trauma and Behaviour — 37
Trauma and Spirituality — 38
Reflections — 39

PART THREE: GATHERING TOOLS — 41

Acknowledge That You Have Been Injured — 43
Safety First — 44
It's about Regaining Some Control — 45
Finding Your Window of "Tolerance" — 46
Sleep Is a Priority — 48
Simplify — 50
Reduce Commitments — 51
Feed Your Body — 52
Just Breathe — 53
Practise Relaxing — 54

You May Need More Rest	55
Sticking to Routines	56
It's Normal to Be Forgetful	57
Accepting Help	58
Accepting Hugs	59
Build Your Support Network	60
Past Traumas May be Triggered	61
What is Dissociation?	62
Memories versus Reliving (Flashbacks)	63
Flashback Triggers	64
Dealing with Flashbacks	65
The 5x Critiquing Rule	67
Physical Pain	68
Alcohol or Substance Use	69
Using Distractions	70
Self-Soothing	71
Staying in the Moment	73
Grounding Objects	74
Physical Comforts	75
It's Not Fair	76
Despair	77
The Warrior Inside	78
This Will Take Some Time	79
The Pain Will Pass	80
If the Pain Feels Unbearable…	81
Establishing Safety	82
Develop a Safety Plan	83
Create a Self-Care Box	84
Nighttime Is Often the Hardest	85

This Isn't the Time for Major Decisions	86
Cocooning for Awhile Is Okay	87
It's Okay to Cry	88
Get It Out	89
Find Your Motivation	90
The Internet: Friend or Foe?	91
How Do Your Faith and Spirituality Fit into All of This?	92
Honest Prayer	93
Part of God's Plan?	94
Recognizing Angels	95
Reflections	96

PART FOUR: HEALING AND FINDING YOUR PATHWAY OUT OF THE VALLEY — 97

When Is It Time to Finish the Climb?	99
Your Story Is Sacred	100
Survivor Guilt	101
Taking Stock of the Losses	102
Grief	103
Scheduling Grieving	104
Injured-Not Damaged	105
Practise Compassion	106
Taking Your Circumstances into Account	107
It May Never Make Sense	108
Hindsight Is a Double-Edged Sword	109
Ongoing Depression	110
Persistent Worry	111
Ongoing Anxiety	112
The Question of Medication	113

Transforming Anger	114
Therapeutic Massage	115
Finding Meaning or Purpose	116
Forgive Yourself If Need Be	117
Love Yourself-Shadow and Light	118
Choosing to Forgive Others	119
Choosing Not to Forgive	120
Preparing for Anniversaries	122
Asking More Adaptive Questions	123
Improving Your Self-Talk	124
Celebrate Your Survival	125
Envision Your Future	126
Who Do You Want to Be?	127
Surround Yourself with Positive People	128
Make Time for Things You Enjoy	129
Nature Can Be Healing	130
You Are Not Your Trauma	131
Acknowledge Your Strength	132
You Have Changed	133
Today Is a New Day	134
Time to Live Your Life	135
Life Is an Ongoing Journey	136
Reflections	137

APPENDIX

Additional Resources for Survivors of Trauma	139

Acknowledgements

When I consider the publication of this book, I am aware of the many people who have directly and indirectly been part of its creation.

I would first like to acknowledge the courageous men and women who have allowed me the honour of bearing witness to their trauma stories and to walk with them through parts of the valley. Your sacred stories are imprinted on my heart. Your strength, courage and perseverance continue to humble, amaze and inspire me.

My own personal journey out of the valley was made possible by the support, caring, and understanding of a number of "angels" whom I was blessed to cross paths with at key points in my life. It is these people who, in many cases unknowingly, made my struggle bearable and gave me hope by their acts of kindness, respect and compassion: Michele Quenneville, Sharon Mitchell, Shawna Weingartner, Lou Anne Quinlan-Perfetto, Michele Colwell, Mike Shanahan, David Reaume, Franco Girimonte, Sean Boyle, Joe Caza, Mark Colwell, Brian Noer, Connie Coniglio, Mike Fox, Janet Izumi, Beverly Ulak, Bonnie Young, Carol Saxby, Marg McGill, Judi Johnston, Laura Naumann, Mary Durocher, Susan Alexander, and Dr. Keith Thompson. You will always have a special place in my heart.

I would like to acknowledge and express my gratitude to the Althouse Press Publication Committee and specifically Dr. Greg Dickinson, Dr. Alan Leschied, Katherine Butson, and Brian Bazett. Thank you for understanding the message of this book and for believing in it as a worthwhile resource. Thank you Greg, Brian and Alan for all the time and effort you put into editing and polishing my written work, and for guiding me through the publication process. Thank you also Brian for sharing your talent of creating gentle visual depictions to provide another medium for connection and understanding.

Thank you also to Dr. Ruth Lanius who kindly agreed to write the Foreword. My admiration for your intelligence, work and compassion, is immeasurable.

Nor do I want to forget the first editors of the original draft of the manuscript prior to submission for publication - Brian Johnson, Shawna Weingartner, Sharon Mitchell, Catherine Miller, and Melissa Mask. You provided valuable feedback, asked excellent questions, and offered ongoing encouragement throughout the writing process. Thank you.

Most of all, I would like to thank my family (Brian, Marcus and Aleisha) for their support and patience as I closed myself off to work on this book. I've been touched by, and appreciative of, your unwavering confidence that my book *would* get published. You were my inspiration on my own journey out of the valley. I loved you even before I knew your names. You are the greatest blessing of all.

Foreword

In this book, Shirley Porter eloquently describes what trauma survivors face on the walk through the valley of the shadow of death until they reach recovery, an account that will be exceedingly valuable for clients and therapists alike. Being trapped in this valley can make the traumatized individual feel profoundly isolated, deserted, and rejected. The traumatized person frequently feels alone with experiences that seem unreal and overwhelming to the point of doubting one's existence in this world. How can we, as therapists, reach trauma survivors in such a state of forsakenness? How can we help them to face a therapeutic relationship that can be petrifying, since past relationships were frequently the source of the individual's terror and abuse? Porter's approach to these questions begins with helping traumatized individuals to understand the origin of their symptoms and to see these experiences as a normal response to highly abnormal and traumatizing encounters, thereby decreasing the shame and confusion often associated with these symptoms. She then provides a step-by-step approach to overcoming the overwhelming experiences associated with a variety of traumatic events, including childhood abuse, domestic violence, and military-related experiences.

Throughout the book, survivors of trauma are offered hope and guidance through the recovery process that will eventually lead them out of the valley of the shadow of death. Specific exercises to manage extreme emotions, pain, and distress are discussed, and making meaning of the traumatic past is encouraged to help the traumatized individuals to see themselves in a new light. Traumatized persons are encouraged to persist in their journey to recovery until they see a way out of their suffering. This book offers hope, inspiration, and an escape from the valley of the shadow of death. I hope that it will serve as a source of healing for many individuals who are suffering from the often devastating effects of trauma.

Ruth A. Lanius, MD, PhD

London, Ontario

Preface

I wrote this book to assist trauma survivors as they embark on their journey of healing. Although this guide is not intended to take the place of therapy, it is my experience that there is a great need for a resource that can provide individuals with support between counselling sessions. I hope that this book will act as that resource.

The information on traumatic stress discussed in the book is drawn from what I have learned throughout my years as a scholar and practitioner. This book is informed by the many professional development seminars and conferences I have attended, and a multitude of research papers and books by experts in the field about how trauma affects the mind and body. More than anything, however, it is informed by clinical experience and the lessons I have learned in being present with those who have been on this journey.

Therapist Babette Rothschild's concept of "applying the brakes" (Rothschild, 2011) has been instrumental in my understanding of the importance of ensuring that individuals have access to effective strategies to reduce distress *prior* to starting to address their experience with trauma. Dr. Ruth Lanius's ground-breaking research (Lanius, 2011; Lanius et al., 2001, 2003) using Magnetic Resonance Imaging (MRI) has increasingly sensitized me to the fact that post-traumatic stress symptoms are associated with specific differences in brain activity when individuals with Post Traumatic Stress Disorder (PTSD) are compared with those who have not had a traumatic experience. This information is critical in helping people realize that they are not simply "imagining" their symptoms. Hope is also to be found in research studies documenting evidence of the brain's neuroplasticity and its ability to adapt and create new neural pathways that aid in coping. The therapies that I list under "Therapies That Work" are those that have been extensively researched and found to be the most effective in treating traumatic stress symptoms. These include the associated symptoms of depression and anxiety that are frequently part of an overall stress reaction.

In this book I favour therapeutic tools based on Cognitive Behavioural Therapy (CBT). CBT has consistently been demonstrated as one of the most effective approaches for dealing with traumatic stress. Simply put, CBT works from the premise that our thoughts, perceptions, and behaviours influence how we feel, and to change how we feel we need to identify and change distorted or negative thought patterns and unhelpful behaviours. Thus, if we target a reduction in an overall level of distress, we focus on making changes at the level of thought. This therapeutic approach is elaborated on in this book under the headings "The 5x Critiquing Rule," "Using Distractions," "Staying in the Moment," "Asking More

Adaptive Questions," "Improving Your Self-Talk," and at the behavioural level, "Accepting Help," "Sleep Is a Priority," "Sticking to Routines," "Self-Soothing," and "Transforming Anger."

In addition to strategies associated with CBT, I focus on *strength mirroring*, which involves reminding yourself of the truths inherent in personal strength, courage, and resilience, all of which can easily be forgotten if you are feeling overwhelmed and in pain. Strength mirroring is implicated in the discussions in the sections entitled "You Are a Survivor," "Being Strong Doesn't Mean You Aren't Exhausted," "The Warrior Inside," "Love Yourself-Shadow and Light," and "You Are Not Your Trauma."

You will likely notice that this book is not tailored to any specific group of trauma survivors such as veterans of war or survivors of childhood abuse or domestic violence. That was purposefully done for one simple reason: regardless of the cause of traumatic stress reactions, trauma affects the mind and body in so many similar ways. The pain can be, in a word, debilitating. For some, the social, emotional, physical, and spiritual costs can prove to be unbearable. Although when working with clients I tailor therapeutic tools and interventions according to individual need, the essential ingredients of trauma and the stabilization and healing strategies that I select are much the same regardless of the cause of the trauma. So, this book is designed to be helpful to all survivors of trauma, no matter what its origin.

Finally, this book, like your climb out of the Valley, invites you to be interactive. At the end of each of the four Parts, you will find a section entitled "Reflections." You will maximize what you get out of this book—and hopefully its impact on your healing journey—by taking up the invitation to write down your reflections on the questions provided there as well as on those posed within the sections of each Part.

References

Lanius, R. A. (2011, October). "Self-reflections, mindfulness, and the traumatized self: Clinical and neurobiological perspectives." Paper presented at the Brain, Mind & Body: Trauma, Neurobiology and the Healing Relationship Conference, the University of Western Ontario, London, Canada.

Lanius, R. A., Williamson, P. C., Densmore, M., Boksman, K., Gupta, M. A., Neufeld, R. W. J., Gati, J. S., & Menon, R. S. (2001). Neural correlates of traumatic memories in posttraumatic stress disorder: A functional MRI investigation. *American Journal of Psychiatry, 158*(11), 1920–1922.

Lanius, R. A., Williamson, P. C., Hopper, J., Densmore, M., Boksman, K., Gupta, M. A., Neufeld, R. W. J., Gati, J. S., & Menon, R. S. (2003). Recall of emotional states in posttraumatic stress disorder: An fMRI investigation. *Biological Psychiatry, 53*(3), 204–210.

Rothschild, B. (2011). Introduction: 10 foundations for safe trauma therapy. In B. Rothschild (Ed.), *Trauma essentials* (pp. 13–16). New York: W.W. Norton.

An Introduction to the Valley

To say that trauma and resultant traumatic stress reactions are unsettling would be a gross understatement. Traumatic experiences, by their nature, can disrupt and overwhelm body, mind, and spirit. If traumatic stress reactions follow and are not appropriately treated, this sense of disruption can continue and cause lasting injury and pain.

When clients who are struggling with traumatic stress reactions come to me for counselling, they are often frustrated and confused about why they are experiencing such distress. Some are aware of the relationship between their symptoms and a previous traumatic experience. Others are not, and it comes to light only when we explore the time at which their symptoms first became an issue. Most clients do not understand how an experience from the past continues to affect their daily lives in such negative and significant ways.

Throughout my career I have struggled to find a visual metaphor to explain traumatic stress to my clients. I wanted to find an image that could make something as complicated as trauma more easily understood. I have often heard the counselling process referred to as a journey. This seems to be an image that works for many people. However, it seems to be inadequate in the context of trauma because it does not fully reflect the true nature and depth of the darkness and despair. I needed something more. I found my image while reading the 23rd Psalm, which begins, "The Lord is My Shepherd...." The psalmist, David, refers to a place known as "the valley of the shadow of death." The journey of sufferers of traumatic stress begins at the entrance to the valley of the shadow of death-which I simply call the "Valley." This Valley is a dark and desolate place that exists in the shadow of some kind of significant ending-a real or symbolic death. In this place you are apt to feel a profound sense of loneliness, despair, and hopelessness. You might struggle to think clearly. Your old coping strategies do not seem to work as well as you hoped they would. You are probably exhausted and feeling deep despair. There are no obvious pathways out of the Valley. The terrain looks treacherous and foreboding. It is difficult to know where to begin.

In the 23rd Psalm David sings about a "walk" through the valley of the shadow of death. Unfortunately, for those suffering from traumatic stress, their stay in the Valley can be much longer than a walk. For some, it becomes a primary residence in which they are trapped for weeks, months, years, and even decades-with no apparent way out. No one should have to live in the Valley indefinitely.

My job as a therapist is to help my clients to become oriented to their surroundings in the Valley and to understand how they arrived there. I also strive to make them aware of the challenges they are likely to face, equip them with the tools and strategies they will need to begin the arduous journey toward finding their way out, and accompany them as a guide and support as they find and then ascend the pathways that will lead them out of the Valley.

This book will offer some of these same supports to you. I hope you find them helpful.

PART ONE

FIRST THINGS FIRST

You have found yourself in the Valley. Maybe you have just arrived or maybe you have been there for a very long time. In either case it is not a pleasant experience, and you are no doubt anxious to find a way out.

It is important to get a few things clear from the outset. First, the fact that you find yourself in the Valley is not the result of a character flaw or weakness on your part. Traumatic stress symptoms are a common, *normal* reaction to traumatic events. Second, to navigate the terrain and find your way out you are going to need professional help. And, finally, there are times when being in the Valley causes some people such despair that their thoughts turn to suicide. Usually this is because they want the pain to stop and cannot fathom another way to escape it. I assure you, there is another way. However, until you can believe this yourself, it will be important to allow other people in your life to hold onto this hope for you.

This Part deals with these important areas, with a special emphasis on acknowledging and normalizing your injuries, as well as ensuring your immediate safety.

"I don't understand what's happening to me. I feel like I'm losing it."

You Are Not Losing Your Mind

Experiencing what may seem to be extreme symptoms following an extreme (i.e., traumatic) event is normal. Trauma can affect your mind, body, emotions, behaviour, and spirit. These symptoms are a signal that you have been wounded and your mind and body are requesting that these wounds be attended to.

Speaking to a professional about your symptoms can reassure you and help normalize what you are going through.

In speaking with others who have gone through something similar, you will likely notice that not everyone experiences exactly the same symptoms. However, knowing that others are struggling, too, may help you to see that you are not alone. It might also provide opportunities to share healthy coping strategies that may help you begin to stabilize.

"What's wrong with me? Why can't I just get over this?"

This Is Not about a Character Flaw

I often find myself needing to clarify a few very important things with clients. They typically include the following assurances and advice:

- This is not about how capable you are.
- This is not about weakness.
- This is not about integrity or character.
- When people have been wounded, they hurt. You have been wounded. You hurt.
- Just because you might not be able to see the injury with your eyes does not mean it is not real and significant.
- Be gentle with yourself. Adding unnecessary guilt or blame will hamper the healing process.

"This is hard. I'm struggling."

You Are a Survivor

Although when you are beginning therapy you may not wholeheartedly believe the following statements are true, you are being asked to be at least open to the *possibility* that they are:

- You have survived the *impossible* already.
- The trauma is over.
- You are safe now. You made it.
- You are adaptable, strong, and resilient. Your body and mind have worked very hard to allow you to make it to this point. Now they will work to help you heal.
- You *will* find your way out of the Valley. Others will help you. You must be open to allowing them to help.
- You are an amazing being.

"When will things be normal again?"

The Journey to Healing

Individual time frames for healing vary. There is no deadline. Each person heals at his or her own pace.

This journey usually involves:
- understanding trauma
- acknowledging your traumatic stress reactions
- gathering tools to cope and reduce distress
- healing and finding your pathway out of the Valley

This is not a linear journey. At times you will feel as if you are going three steps forward and two steps back. Sometimes you will need to return to an old injury to heal at a deeper level. However, it is important to remember that you never truly go backward. Each day you learn something new and move forward.

This is a journey you must take in order to reclaim your life.

"Isn't there a list of things I can check off to get through this?"

An Individual Journey

Healing from trauma is an individual journey.

Just as you are a unique individual with your own personal history and experience of trauma, so too will your map of healing be your own.

Unfortunately, the map is not pre-made. You and your therapist will have to figure out the paths that will make up your journey as you come to understand how the trauma has affected you and what you need to heal.

No one strategy or therapy comprises the entire healing journey for a person.

Your journey will require distress reduction and coping tools, as well as healing interventions. When used altogether, these tools and interventions will provide you with a means of reclaiming your life.

"I don't want to burden anyone else with this."

This Is BIG-Accept Help!

No one should have to do this work alone. Part of the injury associated with trauma is its ability to make you feel isolated and different. The healing process for most people involves accepting help and working with others to get through it.

Doctors, psychologists, psychotherapists, social workers, and counsellors are available to help you. Find one with whom you feel comfortable and who specializes in working with trauma survivors.

There are also a number of support groups for individuals who have survived specific types of trauma (e.g., war, domestic abuse, sexual assault). Find a group with whom you can connect.

Let your loved ones know what you are going through. Tell them what you need. Do not expect them to know. If you are not sure what you need, discuss it with them. Answers will come.

"How do I find someone to talk to?"

Finding a Therapist

One of the best predictors of client success is the client's perception of the therapeutic alliance forged with his or her therapist (i.e., the degree to which the client is comfortable with the therapist, feels safe in the relationship, and believes the therapist is an ally in achieving the desired goals). Thus, it is essential to find a therapist with whom you are comfortable and who you feel understands you.

There are several types of professionals who provide psychotherapy and counselling, including physicians, psychiatrists, counsellors, psychotherapists, and social workers. Check the credentials of counsellors and psychotherapists with provincial or state licensing bodies because in some jurisdictions these titles may be used by anyone, regardless of training or accreditation.

Whichever professional you choose, ensure the person has some *specialization* in working with survivors of trauma.

"What kinds of therapies work? I want to get this over with as quickly as possible."

Therapies That Work

There are evidence-based therapies that are used predominantly in trauma work because they have proven to be effective.[1] When considering a therapist, you may want to ask whether he or she uses any of the following therapies.

Individual Trauma Focused Cognitive Behavioural Therapy (TFCBT)

This type of therapy uses a variety of cognitive and behavioural strategies to change some of the ways you think and behave in order to help reduce your distress and improve your coping abilities. During this therapy there is a focus on memories of the traumatic event to help you to come to terms with them.

Non-Trauma Focused Cognitive Behavioural Therapy (Non-TFCBT)

This type of therapy, although not focusing directly on memories of trauma, also uses a variety of cognitive and behavioural strategies to help change ways of thinking and acting in order to reduce your distress and help you to better cope.

---

1 Bisson, Jonathan I., Roberts, Neil P., Andrew, Martin, Cooper, Rosalind, & Lewis, Catrin. 2013. *Psychological therapies for chronic post-traumatic stress disorder (PTSD) in adults.* The Cochrane Library online: http://onlinelibrary.wiley.com/doi/10.1002/14651858.CD003388.pub4/abstract

Group TFCBT

This therapy uses the same strategies as TFCBT but it is done in a group setting.

Eye Movement Desensitization and Reprocessing (EMDR)

In EMDR, the therapist uses one of a number of techniques to guide your eye movements from side to side, while you recall the worst parts of your traumatic experience (i.e., visually, emotionally, physically, and thoughts related to the experience). This therapy can assist you in reprocessing the memory in such a way that negative emotions and beliefs related to the event are replaced with an absence of distress and more positive beliefs about yourself.

"I feel physically numb, like my body isn't mine."

Other Interventions That Might Help

Following trauma, it is not uncommon to feel disconnected from your body. Strategies that help reconnect you with your body can also help to anchor you in the present moment.

Many trauma survivors have reported experiencing relief from the following interventions and activities:

- registered massage therapy
- yoga
- acupuncture
- meditation

"I've never been to a counsellor before. What's going to happen?"

What Can You Expect from Your Therapist?

Your therapist will approach the counselling process from his or her own personal and professional backgrounds.

Regardless of the theory that your therapist employs, you can expect:

- information about how the therapist works, including his or her theory of trauma counselling and an overview of each of your responsibilities in this process
- an environment that feels comfortable, safe, and respectful-with clear boundaries (i.e., crisis protocol, hours of availability, fees, cancellation policy)
- confidentiality-with limitations clearly explained
- a supportive, professional, and non-judgmental relationship in which the focus is on you
- professional knowledge and understanding of normal trauma reactions
- knowledge of evidence-based strategies to assist you with stabilization, coping, and healing from trauma

"But I'm the one that people come to for help. I should be able to do this by myself."

If You Are Usually the Protector/Helper...

If you are usually the one to whom others come for help, accepting help may be a struggle, but it is very important that you learn how to do it.

Ask yourself how you feel about the people you have helped in your life. Do you think they were weak or inferior? Or, do you just feel honoured that they trusted you enough to let you help?

Asking for help is a sign of strength and character. It involves acknowledging the fact that none of us knows everything there is to know in this life, and that when we work together in addressing challenges, we are stronger.

The bottom line is that there are times in life when we will be the helpers and other times when we will be the ones needing help. And, there may even be times when we are both of these at the very same time.

"I don't feel strong."

Being Strong Doesn't Mean You Aren't Exhausted

You survived the trauma. That took strength and resiliency.

You are also surviving after-trauma symptoms, which, by their very nature, can be as overwhelming as the trauma itself.

Strength and courage have been required of you every day following the trauma to do what is needed in order to cope and begin to heal.

Surviving, coping, and healing are exhausting work.

Being strong does not mean that you will not be exhausted, frustrated, or feeling overwhelmed at times on this journey. Being strong means that, *despite all of the challenges, you keep going*-even if sometimes you feel like you are barely hanging on. The fact that you continue to strive for healing demonstrates your tremendous strength and resiliency.

"I have thoughts about ending it all. I don't want to do this anymore."

If You Are Suicidal…

If you are experiencing suicidal thoughts and believe you may follow through on them, **seek medical assistance immediately!**

Unfortunately, despair and hopelessness are common trauma responses. These symptoms can make it nearly impossible to recall better times and to believe that they will return.

Suicidal thoughts and intentions are a signal that you are finding the pain overwhelming and want it to stop.

Remind yourself that, in this state, you are not thinking rationally.

You *are* working toward making the pain stop. It will happen. It just takes time.

Remember that you have been wounded and require attention. You do not need to go through this alone. There are people and organizations that can help. Allow them to help you.

Once you find your supports and the tools that work for you to manage distress, it will get easier. Ask for help from others AND from your own warrior spirit within (p. 78).

Reflections

1. What do you think about the idea of accepting help from others? What physical and emotional reactions do you have to this idea?
2. What thoughts or ideas might help you to be more open to accepting professional support and offers of assistance from friends and family during this difficult time?

Use the space below to write down your reflections on these questions as well as others posed in the sections in this Part.

PART TWO

UNDERSTANDING TRAUMA

You probably have some idea which traumatic event or series of events landed you in the Valley. What you might be wondering about is why you have not yet fully recovered from the experience.

To prepare for your climb out of the Valley, you need to understand what has happened to you and how it has affected you. Knowledge is an important tool in your journey. It can help you to get your bearings and establish some footholds in the Valley.

This Part is intended to help you to understand trauma, including what types of experiences can cause traumatic stress responses, how people tend to react during traumatic situations, and the range of normal reactions following trauma.

We know that trauma can affect the mind and body in significant ways and leave people with a variety of ongoing physical, emotional, cognitive, behavioural, and spiritual symptoms that interfere with functioning and relationships in everyday life. It is important to notice your symptoms and recognize that they are messages from your mind and body, letting you know that you have been injured and that the injuries require attention. You can take some comfort in understanding that these symptoms are within the range of normal trauma responses and that, with time and the appropriate therapy, most will disappear.

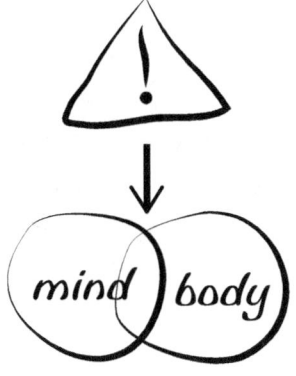

"I've heard the word 'trauma' before, but I thought it referred only to physical injury."

What Is a Trauma?

A *traumatic incident* is defined as one in which a person:

- perceives a significant threat of death or serious injury to him- or herself or someone else
- has a response of horror, fear, and/or a sense of helplessness
- is temporarily overwhelmed, such that his or her normal coping strategies for dealing with stressors feel, or indeed are, inadequate

Trauma reaction is first and foremost a physical reaction. It begins in the brain with a flood of stress hormones that prepare the body to take action in the form of flight, freezing, fighting, submitting, or automatic responses. The response chosen in the thick of the moment will be based on instinctive impulses, which are focused on survival.

In a state of extreme stress that accompanies trauma, the part of the brain that shuts off the warning bell for danger may be so overwhelmed that it is unable to receive the signal that tells it when the danger has passed. When this occurs, the individual stays in a state of hyperarousal. This state is what leads to traumatic stress reaction symptoms.

When the traumatic memory is not appropriately encoded in time (i.e., with a beginning, middle, and *end*), the body and mind continue to be oversensitive to, and triggered by, cues in the present environment that are reminders of the trauma. The individual continues to live in a state of hyperarousal and responds in survival mode even long after the real danger has passed.

There are two types of trauma:

1. *Single Incident Trauma*

    Examples include witnessing someone being killed or badly injured; being a victim of a natural disaster; being involved in a serious car accident; being the victim of rape, another violent crime, or a terrorist act.

2. *Complex Trauma* (occurs over a longer period of time)

    Examples include domestic violence; childhood physical/sexual abuse; combat exposure; internment as a prisoner of war.

"What exactly is PTSD?"

Post-Traumatic Stress Disorder (PTSD)

PTSD[1] might be diagnosed by psychologists, psychiatrists, or other health professionals in situations in which individuals have experienced a traumatic incident in which they believe they or another person was at risk of serious injury or death, and their reaction was horror, terror, and/or helplessness. Additionally, the following criteria must be met:

- intrusive reliving of the event continues to occur (e.g., through nightmares, night terrors, daydreams, flashbacks)
- avoidance or numbing strategies are being used to reduce exposure to reminders of the trauma (e.g., avoiding the place or people connected to the trauma, forgetting important details of the trauma)
- a continuing state of hyperarousal exists (e.g., insomnia, irritability, concentration difficulties, jumpiness)
- this continuing distress negatively affects the person's life (i.e., school, work, social, family, etc.)
- symptoms continue for longer than four weeks

---

1   American Psychiatric Association. (2013) *Diagnostic and statistical manual of mental disorders,* (5th ed.). Washington, DC: Author.

"Sometimes to stop the pain, I drink or cut myself."

Complex Post-Traumatic Stress Disorder

Complex PTSD can occur if you were exposed to ongoing, multiple traumas such as childhood abuse or domestic violence. If you survived multiple traumas over a period of time, you might also experience the following symptoms in addition to the PTSD symptoms mentioned previously:

- difficulty managing what feel like overwhelming emotions and related self-destructive behaviours (e.g., self-injury, eating disorders, alcohol or substance abuse, suicidal actions)
- feeling dissociated, disconnected from your body, or spaced out, and/or having amnesia related to the traumatic events
- seeing yourself very negatively - feeling helpless, guilty, shameful, damaged, unworthy, and/or different
- finding it difficult or impossible to trust others (you might also continue to be victimized by others, or alternatively take on the role of victimizing others)
- ongoing physical symptoms that are difficult to diagnose and treat such as chronic pain, stomach issues, headaches, etc.
- feelings of despair and loss of hope and the inability to find meaning in life

---

Adapted from: Herman, J. (1997). *Trauma and Recovery*. New York: Basic Books.

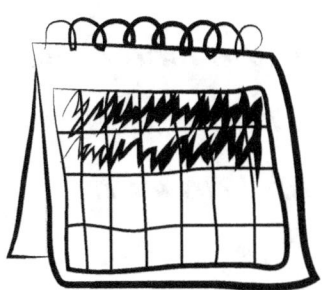

"The trauma happened two weeks ago but I still can't sleep and I see it happening over and over again in my mind. Do I have PTSD?"

Acute Stress Response

Some trauma reactions happen within hours of an incident. Others appear after a few days. Those that occur *within the first four weeks* following a traumatic event are referred to as acute stress responses.

Acute Stress Disorder shares common criteria with PTSD, and differs only with respect to the time frame involved and the added criterion that, during or soon after the event, the individual experiences symptoms of dissociation (e.g., feelings of numbness, being dazed, forgetting important parts of the incident).

For the majority of people, acute stress symptoms will peak in intensity during the first few weeks following the trauma and then diminish, eventually disappearing by the fourth week.

The strategies for coping with acute stress are the same as those used for PTSD.

Individuals who continue to experience acute stress symptoms beyond four weeks should be professionally assessed for PTSD.

"Does everyone who goes through the same kind of trauma end up with PTSD?"

Factors That Affect the Development of PTSD

What one person experiences as traumatic may not necessarily be experienced in that way by another.

Factors that affect the onset of PTSD include:

- the magnitude and duration of the trauma
- the relationship of the trauma survivor to other victims of the same trauma
- whether the trauma was caused deliberately by another person
- the history of the individual (i.e., exposure to other traumas, chronic medical or psychological illness, and recent or subsequent major life stressors or emotional strain)
- the nature of the relationship between the perpetrator of the trauma and the victim
- the age of the trauma survivor at the time of the trauma
- whether the trauma survivor felt believed and supported if he or she disclosed the trauma

"I'm in a job where I'm exposed to a lot of trauma. What can I do to protect myself?"

Protective Factors

Although the following factors will not guarantee that a person will not develop traumatic stress symptoms, they can increase resiliency and healing:

- the use of adaptive coping strategies in dealing with stress on a daily basis (e.g., a balanced life, exercise, good nutrition, supportive relationships)
- a sense of competency in life
- hope regarding the future
- physical health
- intelligence
- the support of peers, friends, workmates, and family

"Are there many people with PTSD? Sometimes I feel like I'm the only one."

The Prevalence of Trauma

Among the general population, approximately 60% of men and 50% of women report at least one traumatic event at some point in their lives. Of these, about 5% of men and 10% of women go on to develop PTSD. This means that 7% to 8% of the population will have PTSD during their lifetimes[1].

The good news is that most people recover from initial traumatic stress symptoms within a few weeks.

For those who continue to suffer from trauma symptoms beyond the initial four-week period, it is essential to obtain professional help.

---

[1] The incidence is somewhat greater in the military and other professions. For U.S data, see U.S. Department of Veterans Affairs, National Center for PTSD. (2014, October 10). *How common is PTSD?* Retrieved from http://www.ptsd.va.gov/public/PTSD-overview/basics/how-common-is-ptsd.asp. There is little reason to believe that the prevalence of PTSD in Canada is significantly different: see Canadian Mental Health Association, British Columbia Division. (2013). Post-Traumatic Stress Disorder. Retrieved from http://www.cmha.bc.ca/get-informed/mental-health-information/ptsd.

"I don't understand why I froze. That's not like me."

The Scope of Trauma Response

During the occurrence of the traumatic event the body responds *instinctively*, though not necessarily rationally, to perceived threats in an attempt to increase chances for survival.

Typical responses include:
- crying
- flight - running away from the threat
- freezing - the inability to move (sometimes involving the inability to speak and/or amnesia during the most stressful part of the traumatic event)
- fighting - actively engaging with or against the threat
- submission
- automatic responses - as a result of training (e.g., military or emergency response procedures)

"I can't stop thinking about it."

Reducing Distress Is the Priority

When the body is flooded with stress hormones and adrenalin as a response to trauma, a state of hyperarousal occurs.

In this intense state of distress and narrowed alertness, trauma memories may become seared into the brain, causing acute stress symptoms to develop.

The primary task of psychological first responders (e.g., counsellors, psychologists) is to help trauma sufferers reduce the level of distress they are experiencing in an attempt to prevent the onset of traumatic stress symptoms and the development of PTSD.

The body and mind need to sense and express a resolution to the trauma, like a big sigh that is felt throughout the body and the mind, in order for the trauma and threat to be experienced as truly finished. This allows the body and the mind to relax and reset.

"How can this be normal?"

Post-Trauma Responses

It is not unusual for people to experience a variety of stress symptoms following a traumatic incident.

Trauma symptoms can affect all aspects of one's being:

- physical
- emotional
- cognitive
- behavioural
- spiritual

Trauma responses, however, vary from person to person. Not everyone experiences every symptom. Not every symptom is experienced in exactly the same way or with the same degree of intensity.

"I feel awful. I'm always exhausted and my body hurts all over."

Trauma and Your Body

Following trauma, if hyperarousal is maintained, the body will often express its distress through physical symptoms. Whatever a person's normal physical vulnerabilities to stress may be, trauma reactions tend to be noticed there first and may expand to include:

- fatigue or exhaustion
- body aches
- nausea and/or vomiting
- sweating
- breathing difficulties
- muscle tremors
- chills
- dizziness
- weakness

"I feel numb most of the time. Other than that I get angry over little things that never bothered me before."

Trauma and Emotions

Trauma can cause emotional numbness and significant distress. These are some of the more common emotional reactions:

- agitation
- anger/rage
- irritability
- sadness
- despair
- guilt
- hopelessness
- fear/terror
- depression
- grief
- shame

"I'm having a hard time concentrating. I'm forgetting all kinds of things and am having a hard time making even simple decisions."

Trauma and Thinking

Trauma can overload your ability to think clearly, rationally, and quickly. Common responses include:

- poor concentration and memory
- difficulty with decision making
- poor problem solving
- confusion
- hypervigilance (constant scanning of surroundings for possible threats)
- nightmares and/or night terrors
- the reliving of the event over and over in your mind
- suicidal thoughts

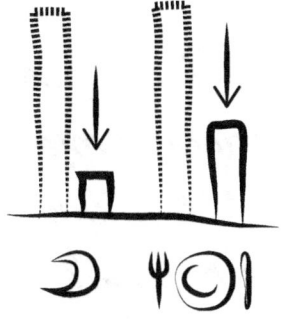

"I can't sleep at all and I'm not hungry. I've lost so much weight in the past few weeks that my clothes don't fit anymore."

Trauma and Behaviour

With the mind and body on overload, behavioural changes are often noticed. Some of the more commonly reported changes may include:

- changes* in sleep patterns
- changes* in appetite
- changes in appearance - others may comment that you look different
- an increase in alcohol consumption or substance abuse
- an increase in risk-taking behaviour (e.g., starting fights, impaired driving, promiscuous behaviour including unprotected sex)
- emotional outbursts
- being easily startled
- social withdrawal or isolation

*i.e., significantly more or less than that which is usual for you

"Ever since this happened I've been questioning my faith. How could God have allowed this to happen?"

Trauma and Spirituality

Individuals who believe in God or a Higher Power often experience a crisis of faith following trauma. This crisis may be temporary or prolonged and may include:

- feeling betrayal, shame, and/or guilt
- feeling abandoned
- anger
- despair
- questioning
- confusion
- searching for meaning
- a significant increase or decrease in time spent in prayer

We will return later to the role and place of spirituality in healing from trauma.

Reflections

1. What facts about trauma would be helpful to remember as you heal?
2. How has trauma affected your body? Emotions? Thoughts? Behaviours? Spirituality?
3. Which symptoms are causing the most distress in your life right now?

Use the space below to write down your reflections on these questions as well as others posed in the sections in this Part.

PART THREE

GATHERING TOOLS

Now that you have some understanding of how you arrived in the Valley and what to expect in terms of the typical challenges that you might experience there, it is time to help you to gather tools for the journey ahead. The Valley has its own obstacles. You need to be prepared for them.

This Part is about acknowledging and tending to the injuries you have sustained. It is about rest, healing, safety, and more generally, about giving yourself the time, space, and supports you need to allow yourself to begin to heal. This part of the journey is about focusing on what you need *in the present moment*. Mostly, it is concerned with stabilization.

The tools in this Part can provide you with the ability not only to reduce your overall distress level, but also to increase your tolerance for distress when it arises. It will be important to identify, try out, and implement those tools that help to reduce your distress level on a daily basis. Recognize that one tool alone will not be *the* answer to get you through the rough spots. One strategy may reduce your stress by 6%, another by 5%, and another by 9%; but, if they are used together, you might see a 20% reduction in distress, which can make a big difference. Regularly using these tools can give you a sense of power and control over your traumatic stress reactions so that you no longer feel helpless and frightened by them.

The other important thing to remember is that in utilizing these tools you are teaching your mind and body new ways to respond to distress. It will take some time to become familiar with the tools and to learn how to use them. Be patient with yourself.

"The injuries that hurt the most are the ones that people can't see."

Acknowledge That You Have Been Injured

Denying that you have been emotionally injured by trauma, in the face of clear trauma symptoms and reactions, will only slow the healing process.

Just because you cannot see the injuries with your eyes does not mean they are not real. The effects of acute stress disorder and PTSD are well documented in the research literature.

The first step is to take note of your symptoms and when they started. Are they improving or worsening? If they are worsening and interfering with your daily life, seek professional help without delay.

There are things you can do to help yourself heal - starting with acknowledging that you have been injured.

"It's not over."

Safety First

Before you can deal effectively with trauma, it needs to be *in the past*. It cannot be a recurring part of your life. If you are living in an abusive relationship, you need to safely exit that relationship and access support to exit it, or get effective help to change it.

If you are truly unsafe in your daily life, you will (and wisely so) be in a defensive posture, and will need to continue to be on guard and intensely alert to your surroundings in order to survive ongoing threats. This is not a posture that will allow you to deal effectively with past trauma.

The external threat of the recurring trauma needs to be eliminated or minimized in order for you to let down your guard enough to allow you to begin to understand the reasons for the defences you have erected, to recognize how they are impacting your daily life, and to take steps to heal.

You need to establish a sense of safety, not only emotionally with the people who will help you to do this, but also physically in your day-to-day surroundings. Are you safe? If not, what needs to change for you to feel safe enough to start to let your guard down?

"Since that day, I feel as if my life has been turned upside down and things are out of control."

It's about Regaining Some Control

During trauma, the situation *is* out of your control and you are extremely vulnerable. It is a terrifying and overwhelming experience. After the traumatic event itself has ended, the feelings of helplessness and lack of control need to be rectified.

The first goal following trauma is stabilization, which means helping you to regain a sense of control over your symptoms and, thus, your life. This involves using practical cognitive and behavioural strategies to reduce your level of distress. These strategies will take some effort and practice but they are well worth it. You will find a number of these strategies in the pages that follow.

Taking control by trying out coping strategies and tailoring them, if need be, to find what works for you, is a step that you will need to make in order to move forward in your healing journey. It will require effort on your part.

"At times I feel nothing at all."

Finding Your "Window of Tolerance"

In the throes of traumatic stress reactions, you will probably alternate between times when you are feeling overwhelming emotion and others when you are dealing with unbearable numbness.

Some people in extreme distress will be drawn to use alcohol, drugs, self-injury, or other high-risk behaviours to try to move back into their window of tolerance. The goal in this section is not only to help you to find healthy and effective tools to reduce the intensity of these emotional states and to make them more tolerable, but also to widen your window of tolerance.

The Window of Tolerance[1] can be a very helpful concept to understand.

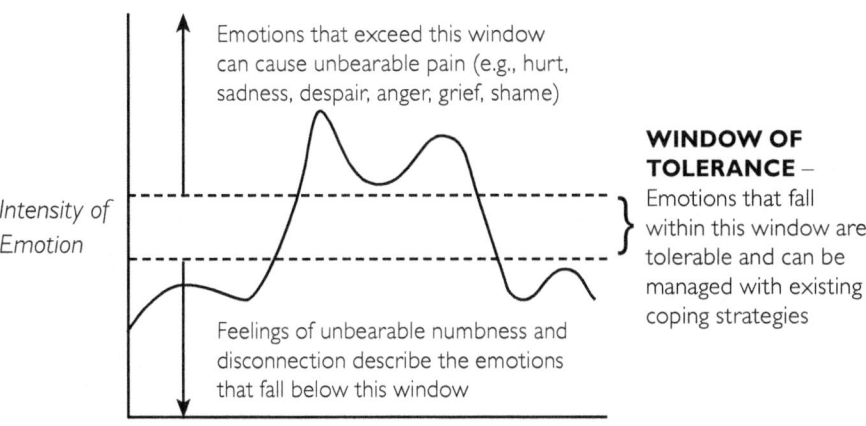

---

[1] This phrase is first used by Daniel J. Seigel in *The Developing Mind: How Relationships and the Brain Interact to Shape Who We Are*. New York: Guilford Press, 1999, p. 253. The application of the concept of window of tolerance to trauma was developed by Pat Ogden, Kekuni Minton and Clare Pain, in *Trauma and the Body: A Sensorimotor Approach to Psychotherapy*. New York: Norton.

"I can't remember the last time I slept for more than a few hours."

Sleep Is a Priority

Prolonged sleep disturbance must be addressed.

Sleep deprivation is associated with increased stress response. It will affect your thinking, mood, emotions, and body, often mimicking symptoms of PTSD.

You need sleep to have the strength to enact the coping strategies and exit map that you create.

Here are some suggestions for trying to improve sleep:

- avoid napping during the day
- reduce or eliminate caffeine intake, especially in the afternoon or early evening
- engage in physical activity in the early part of your day
- just prior to bedtime, do not read books or watch television programs or movies that contain violence or that elicit fear, helplessness, or horror

- go to bed only when sleepy, and if you toss and turn, get up and leave your room. Do a boring activity for 20 minutes (e.g., word search, solitaire with cards), then try again to sleep
- listen to relaxing music or practise relaxation exercises in the evening
- get up at the same time each day

"It's all too much right now."

Simplify

In the aftermath of trauma, it may be wise to pause to see what the next short period of time will hold for you and how you might simplify your life during this time.

Are there some responsibilities that you can hand off to others for a while to give yourself more time and energy for coping and healing?

Are there people who would be willing to help out with some of your daily responsibilities (e.g., taking care of your children for a few hours so you can get some rest, preparing a meal for you)?

What tasks on your "to-do" list can wait?

You have likely heard the phrase "Keep it simple." Now is a very good time to put it into practice.

"My life was so busy before this happened! Now it seems impossible to keep up."

Reduce Commitments

Coping with the aftermath of trauma is a strenuous undertaking in and of itself.

Now is not the time to take on additional commitments at work or in your personal life.

In fact, if at all possible, it may be a good idea to relinquish or delegate some of those commitments to others until you are not feeling so overwhelmed.

If you are struggling to keep up with work and are unsuccessful at reducing commitments, you may wish to speak with your physician about setting up workplace accommodations.

Right now, healing is your top priority.

 *"I'm craving comfort foods."*

Feed Your Body

When your body is under stress it requires healthy foods to sustain it and assist with healing - both physically and emotionally. Fresh fruits and vegetables, whole grains, and lean meats will provide your body with the fuel it needs to cope.

If your stomach is upset, you may want to try five or six small meals a day instead of three large ones.

A common error made by individuals dealing with traumatic stress reactions is to skip meals. Unfortunately, this places additional stress on an already over-stressed body and can intensify your symptoms.

It is also important to ensure that you drink plenty of water. The stress hormone overload caused by the initial trauma, and possibly triggered by ongoing traumatic stress reactions, requires water to flush it from your body.

Although junk food may be tempting during times of high stress, try to limit your intake of it by making healthy food choices most of the time.

"There are times when I get so scared that I forget to breathe."

Just Breathe

Focusing on your breathing is a quick and simple way to calm yourself down and clear your mind. It can also connect you to your body and help you feel a sense of control over your physical state.

Here is a simple exercise you can try. Find a place where you feel comfortable and close your eyes or focus on the floor in front of you. Then pay attention to your breathing. Do not change it. Just notice it. Try to notice the point at which exhaling changes to inhaling. Focus on this for about a minute.

This exercise may be helpful to you if you are having difficulty calming your mind enough to go to sleep at night. You may also want to try it with some modifications, such as breathing in through your nose and out through your mouth, and/or breathing deeply into your abdomen. You could also focus on breathing out "pain" or "tension" and breathing in "relaxation."

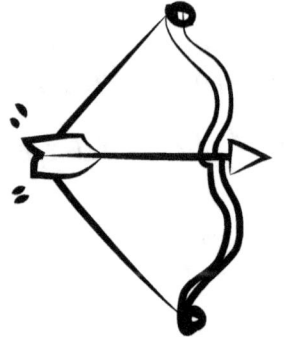

"My muscles are always tense. It now seems to be their normal state."

Practise Relaxing

You might have to relearn how to relax following the trauma experience.

During the trauma your muscles were tensed as they readied to do what was necessary for your survival.

If the tension has continued after the fact, you may need to take steps to help your body to relearn relaxation.

Gently stretching tight, sore muscles can help release the tension and remind your body how it feels to relax.

You can also try *progressive relaxation*. It involves lying down in a place where you feel safe. Close your eyes. Begin by concentrating on your breathing. Beginning with muscle groups starting at your feet, tense and hold for five seconds, then gently relax. Do this twice for each muscle group, moving upwards from your feet to your head.

"When I sleep, I still wake up tired."

You May Need More Rest

Coping with the aftermath of trauma is tiring; there is no question about it.

If you were physically injured as well, then you have an additional layer of fatigue to deal with while your body uses its energy to heal and cope with pain.

During this time, you will likely require additional rest. Give yourself this time. It is important to your healing process.

Some people find it helpful to go to bed an hour earlier at night.

Be mindful of the demands you are placing on yourself. Would you expect the same from a friend or loved one who had been through the same thing? If the answer is no, then it is time to rethink the expectations you have of yourself.

You deserve the same degree of empathy and compassion that you would give the important people in your life.

 *"I get up in the morning and don't know where to begin."*

Sticking to Routines

Keeping to your routines as much as possible following the traumatic event can help to re-establish a sense of normalcy in your life.

Routines are predictable and can provide a sense of safety and stability, both of which were painfully absent during the trauma.

Routines can also be helpful in anchoring you in the present moment if you focus on where you are and what you are doing.

Going back to your normal patterns is a way to reaffirm that the traumatic event itself is over, you survived, and your life is moving forward.

"I've been losing things and forgetting appointments. What's wrong with me?"

It's Normal to Be Forgetful

With your mind still diligently trying to digest and process the trauma, your memory may not be all it used to be.

Such memory problems are temporary and to be expected as you learn to cope with traumatic stress reactions.

Try not to get down on yourself.

Write things down in a notebook or personal organizer. Include a task list for each week, broken down by days. Check it regularly.

If you notice you are forgetting what would normally be routine for you (e.g., things that need to be done to get yourself and your children ready for the day, what bills need to be paid when), make a list of these things, too.

Memory aids might take some pressure off you, because you will not have to waste so much energy worrying about forgetting things.

"Lots of people have said to let them know if I need anything, but I don't want to be a burden."

Accepting Help

When friends offer to help, and most of them really would like to help somehow, they may not know what you need. You need to tell them.

Accepting help from others can be quite a challenge, especially if you are independent and used to handling everything quite competently on your own. However, in the aftermath of trauma, accepting help can be a sanity saver.

If your friends or family offer help, consider accepting it.

What would take the edge off just a bit right now? Help with a few errands? A break from the children? Someone to make dinner for you?

Give others the opportunity to help you when you need it. Chances are the time will come when you can return the favour.

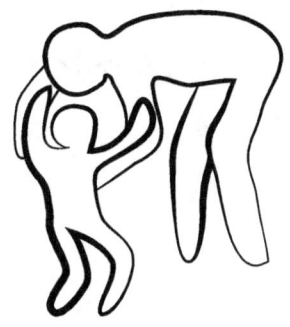

"A hug from my two-year-old son can change everything."

Accepting Hugs

As long as hugs are not a flashback trigger for you, they may be a source of hope, comfort, and healing.

Hugs connect people at the most basic level and convey a number of different messages:

- I'm here for you
- I care about you
- I'm glad to see you
- you will get through this
- you can lean on me

They are a gift to both the giver and the receiver.

Consider giving and receiving hugs to be part of your survival plan and healing process.

"I want to deal with this on my own."

Build Your Support Network

There are times in life when handling a challenging situation on your own may be admirable. This is not one of them.

Dealing effectively with trauma typically involves accepting support from caring and understanding individuals or groups, who may include both professionals and non-professionals.

On the professional side, you should have a connection with, at least, a counsellor who specializes in trauma and a supportive physician.

Non-professionals may include your significant other, family members, friends, and people who have survived similar experiences.

You may also want to connect with community resources or associations that deal with trauma caused by specific circumstances (e.g., sexual assault centres, veterans' groups, domestic violence support groups, bereaved parents' groups).

"Since this event I can't stop thinking about something else that happened years ago."

Past Traumas May Be Triggered

If there are unresolved traumas in your past, your most recent experience may reactivate them.

Painful memories and emotions from your past may resurface. They may even be more intense than those connected with the recent trauma.

Consequently, your feelings and symptoms may be more intense because they are associated with more than one trauma.

The good news is that you can likely work on past and present traumas together. Trauma themes, for better or worse, tend to have a lot of parallels no matter what the content.

Regardless of the number of traumas you are working on, you will still need a self-care plan. The goal remains to reduce distress and help you regain some control over your symptoms.

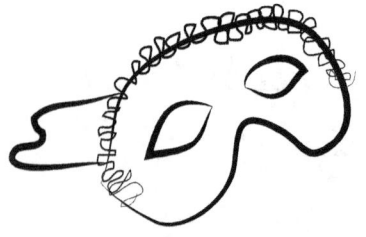

"I can be in a room with people but I'm not really there."

What is *Dissociation*?

Put simply, *dissociation* refers to feeling emotionally and physically split off from oneself.

Some people report having felt as if they had left their bodies during the traumatic incident and were watching the event happen to someone else.

This compartmentalization or splitting off is thought to be a protective action of the mind and body to prevent overload.

If you became dissociative during the trauma, you are more likely to dissociate following the trauma.

Like flashbacks, dissociation can have triggers.

Dissociation may last for a few minutes or for several hours.

If you seem to be losing time in your day (e.g., you look at a clock and realize that a chunk of time has gone by that you do not remember), you might be dissociating.

If you start to become aware of warning signs prior to experiencing dissociation, you can try to avert the dissociation by anchoring yourself in the present moment through your senses.

"I feel like I relive this event several times a day."

Memories versus Reliving (Flashbacks)

Reliving trauma experiences is not like recalling other memories.

Non-trauma memories involve an awareness that you are in the present and remembering something that happened in your past. The emotions connected to the event may or may not be felt. If they are felt, they tend to be less intense than they were at the time the event happened.

Reliving trauma, on the other hand, places you back in the past. You are no longer aware of the present moment. Your body, mind, and emotions relive the event as though it were happening in the here and now.

During flashbacks you return to a state of terror and hyperarousal. Stress hormones flood through your body. Your body readies itself to respond to the perceived threat. However, in the present moment the only threat that actually exists is the one in your mind.

Given how real they seem, flashbacks can understandably cause a great deal of distress.

The goal in coping with flashbacks is to eventually connect with the part of your mind that knows they are only memories and that can remind you that the events themselves are over and not happening again.

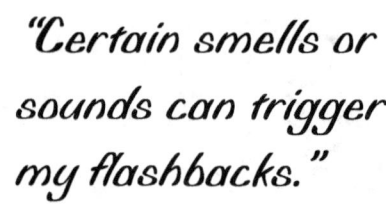

"Certain smells or sounds can trigger my flashbacks."

Flashback Triggers

It is important to figure out what your flashback triggers are so that you can try to limit your exposure to them, at least until you have support and strategies for dealing with them.

Flashback triggers can be just about anything. They can be a specific person or type of person (e.g., body type, occupation). They can be an object or a place. They can be a particular colour, sound, phrase, or smell. Flashbacks can be triggered by touch or pain. They can also be triggered by intense stress or emotion (e.g., terror, despair, rage).

You may want to keep a log of when and where your flashbacks occur. It may also be helpful to write down what was happening immediately prior to the onset of the flashback. This may help you to identify your trigger.

Once you know what your triggers are, you can work with your counsellor to develop strategies to help you to deal with them.

"The flashbacks are brutal. One minute everything is normal. The next I'm back in hell."

Dealing with Flashbacks

Flashbacks can be terrifying. They can jettison you back to some of the worst moments of your life. The sights, sounds, and body sensations can seem horrifically real.

It is important to regain a sense of control when it comes to flashbacks. Here are a few strategies to try:

- Until you have experienced some success in controlling flashbacks, you may want to avoid situations that trigger them. Therefore, as we just discussed, you must pay attention to what triggers them.
- If you feel a flashback coming on, go somewhere where you can experience it safely (i.e., where you won't be open to harm in this heightened vulnerable state). If you have time, try to use your senses (e.g., ask yourself what you see, hear, smell, and feel in the real world) to anchor yourself in the present moment.
- If you can get in touch with the part of yourself that witnesses the flashback (likely the part that's saying, "Not again!"), use this part of your rational mind to remind yourself, "This is not real. It's over. I survived."

- If your flashbacks are visual, you may want to try to imagine that they are playing on a television screen in front of you. Imagine changing the channel to a more peaceful memory. Or, you can turn the television off and focus on what is going on around you. Practising this repeatedly can sometimes extinguish visual flashbacks.
- Can you recall a sense of relief after the traumatic incident was over? If so, it might be helpful to focus on the memory of this instead. How did you feel emotionally and physically when you finally knew the danger was past? Next time a flashback threatens to begin, or when it is finished, remind yourself of the physical and emotional relief you felt when you realized the traumatic experience was over. Try to relive that feeling of relief.

If you do not recall a sense of the trauma being over, and it feels as if it has not stopped, talk to your counsellor about this concern.

If a friend or significant other tends to be around when flashbacks occur, ask him or her to do the following during these episodes:

- NOT touch you
- call your name
- look into your eyes
- gently remind you that the trauma is over and that you are safe and not alone

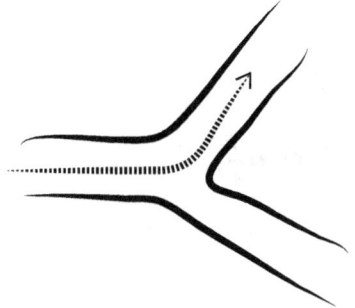

"I spend hours thinking about what ifs."

The 5x Critiquing Rule

It is common after a traumatic event to go over the event in your mind, trying to understand what happened and what you might have done differently to achieve a better outcome.

However, some people get lost in the *what ifs* and can end up spending many hours, days, months, and even years, in this exercise. Obviously there comes a point when *what if* thinking becomes maladaptive.

If you are missing out on today because your time, energy, and thinking are focused endlessly on a past that cannot be altered, then this behaviour needs to be changed.

The 5x (pick a number you like) Critiquing Rule allows you to critique the trauma incident on five occasions, by yourself or with others, to try to determine what you could have done differently. After that (other than in counselling), no longer allow yourself to waste your time on this train of thought.

If you find yourself entertaining *what if* thinking after you have reached your critiquing limit, tell yourself, "That's it. I'm not going down this road anymore," and redirect your focus. It will take some practice, but eventually your mind will give up trying to go there.

"I've been having headaches daily."

Physical Pain

Physical pain that is not a result of physical injury can occur as part of the body's stress response to trauma.

Common trauma reactions involving physical pain include headaches, back pain, stomach aches, intestinal cramps, and other digestive discomfort.

Some people ignore or downplay their pain because they mistakenly believe it is *all in their head.*

Pain is a signal from the body that something is not right and needs to be attended to. As you continue to work at strategies that reduce distress, your physical pain will likely start to decrease.

You may want to try writing journal entries about your pain. Using your non-dominant hand, ask your pain to tell you what it needs, and just write it down without censoring your thoughts. You may be surprised by what you learn.

It is also important to exercise caution when physical pain is involved. Discuss your symptoms with your physician because there is always the possibility that they may not be the result of traumatic stress but have an organic cause that requires medical treatment.

"I've been having a drink every night to settle myself down."

Alcohol or Substance Use

Sometimes people turn to alcohol or prescription or street drugs to escape from or dull painful trauma memories or symptoms. In the short term, this self-medication may seem to provide temporary relief.

However, using alcohol or street drugs, or developing a dependency on prescription drugs, to deal with trauma can have serious negative consequences. It can delay or deter you from finding adaptive, healthy ways to truly gain control over your trauma symptoms. It will also waste your time, energy, and money, all of which would be better invested in healing activities. Moreover, it can set you up for other significant problems and complications in your life (e.g., addiction, legal issues, relationship conflict, work problems).

Your physician has the expertise to oversee your use of appropriate medications, if needed.

Your counsellor can help you to pinpoint the source of the emotional pain that you are trying to escape, and to develop alternative healthy strategies and tools to reduce your distress.

"Sometimes the only way I can forget about it is to get wrapped up in a movie."

Using Distractions

Sometimes, healthy or neutral distractions are needed to give your mind and body a break from thoughts about the trauma.

Examples of distractions include:
- listening to or singing your favourite song
- cleaning
- taking a hot shower or bath
- exercising
- reading
- watching a movie or TV program
- playing a video game
- playing sports
- hanging out with a friend

You need to find some distractions that will work for you. It may be helpful to keep a list, because it can be difficult to think of these things when you are feeling distressed.

"There's something about sitting by the water that gives me a sense of peace."

Self-Soothing

Self-soothing involves calming or providing comfort to yourself through your senses. Here are some examples of how you might try to do this for each of the five senses.

Visual
- look for the richness of colour in nature or a piece of art
- look for patterns in stone or landscape
- notice the sparkle in a child's eyes
- find your favourite shade of green in your surroundings
- colour or paint a picture in vivid colours

Auditory
- listen to relaxing music
- listen to birds chirping
- go to a park and listen to children laughing
- sit beside a river, a lake, or the ocean and listen to the sounds of the water
- notice the sound of your own breathing

Taste
- try a hot, spicy drink like chai tea
- enjoy the warmth of hot chocolate or a flavoured coffee
- bite into fresh fruit while noticing its texture and taste
- chew your favourite gum
- enjoy a favourite food from your childhood

Smell
- light a scented candle
- bake an apple pie or some cookies
- wear your favourite fragrance
- open a window and breathe in the air
- smell flowers

Touch
- have a massage or a pedicure
- pet a dog or a cat
- take a warm bubble bath
- put freshly laundered sheets on your bed
- wear your favourite comfy clothes

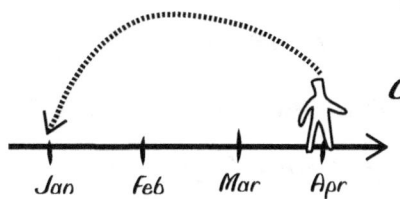

"It seems like my mind is always in the past."

Staying in the Moment

Trauma may not only have stolen part of your past, it may also continue to steal parts of your present.

This is why it is important to do your best to stay in the present moment whenever possible.

Trauma can drag you into a past you have already survived and make you fearful of a future that may never even happen. When this occurs your life in the *now* is lost.

Try to focus on the moment before you right now. What is being asked of you? Use your senses to anchor yourself. What do you see? Hear? Smell?

If you have trouble remembering how to stay in the moment, spend some time with a child or a puppy. They tend to be very good at staying in the present moment and getting the adults around them to do the same!

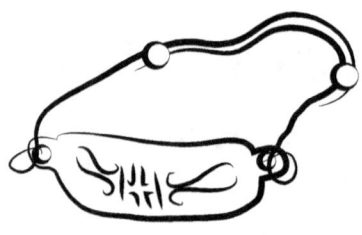

"Whenever I look at this bracelet I remember that someone loves me, believes in me, and needs me. So I have to go on."

Grounding Objects

During the trauma you may have forgotten who you are in terms of your capabilities, qualities, and connections with other people.

After the trauma you may have similar moments of feeling so overwhelmed that you question your ability to handle the situation in front of you.

Grounding objects are things that will help to remind you who you are and what matters to you. They can also help to anchor you in the present moment. You can draw strength and perspective from them.

These objects are usually small and portable so that you can carry them with you wherever you go.

Common grounding objects include pictures of loved ones, a stone or shell from a favourite vacation spot, a piece of jewellery that has sentimental value, and cards and medallions with inspirational sayings written on them.

"When I'm feeling overwhelmed, I just want to get into some comfortable clothes and listen to jazz."

Physical Comforts

Another way to take the edge off trauma reactions is to be mindful of physical comforts.

If you have been feeling especially vulnerable or cold, you may want to consider whether there is a particular sweater or sweatshirt you can wear to give you warmth and comfort.

To help get yourself through a rough day, is there a particular food you could make that you associate with warm and safe memories?

Is there a particular type of music that calms you?

During stressful times in your past, what things gave you healthy physical comforts?

Music, lighting, scents, favourite clothes, specific foods, non-alcoholic drinks - these are some simple, practical ways to provide yourself with comfort and to connect to the present moment.

"Why did this happen to me? It doesn't seem fair."

It's Not Fair

No, it is *not* fair. You did not deserve it, and it is not your fault. You have every right to feel angry about what you have been through and what you are going through now.

Although you did not create this mess, only you can clean it up.

You have a choice to make - here and now. You can feed your anger in such a way that it fuels self-pity and resentment, or you can transform it into motivation and strength that will help you to move forward - toward healing.

How might you deal with the injustice in a healthy way?

"There are times when I don't believe I'll make it through this."

Despair

Despair is one of the most potentially destructive trauma responses. It takes away hope and can plunge you into darkness so thick that you cannot recall a time when it did not envelope your life.

Despair can convince you that all that is left for you are pain and disappointment.

Do not believe it!

Despair is born of terror and paralysis. It is the part of you that wants to curl up in a ball and hide. But, it is not *all* of you.

Despair is a symptom. It is not an accurate reflection of your reality.

There is a warrior/survivor part of you that is even stronger. Despair is trying to make you forget that. Listen for the voice of this strong part of you. Hear its whispers of encouragement and hope.

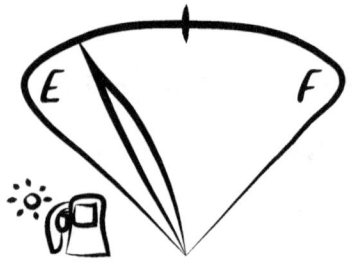

"I don't know what is keeping me going."

The Warrior Inside

Are you aware of the warrior inside you? It is that part of you that allowed you to survive the trauma. It made you do what you needed to do in order to get through the worst moments of your life.

This warrior part of you is your invincible spirit. It is unchanged by trauma. It has a timeless perspective and knows that you, too, are timeless.

It does not give up and sees beyond the challenges facing you to a brighter future.

Listen to your warrior's voice. At first the words will be whispers, but as you listen, your inner hearing will adjust and you will begin to hear more clearly.

Allow the warrior within to be your source of hope and strength. Hear its encouragement. Trust its direction. It is the wisest and strongest part of you.

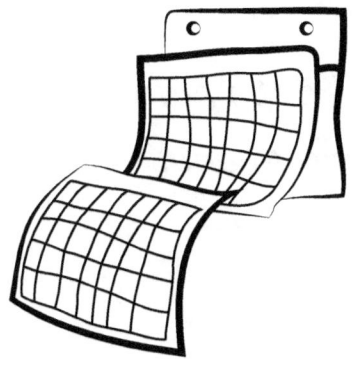

"I should be over this by now."

This Will Take Some Time

Be patient with yourself. This will take some time.

It can be frustrating going through this process. In the midst of it, it can seem like it is never-ending. You are, however, moving forward with each passing day.

Losses have to be grieved. Physical and emotional injuries have to be attended to.

Do not fight the timing. Do not set deadlines for your healing. Healing does not happen on a predetermined schedule. It will happen in its own time.

If you trust and work with the process, instead of against it, it will go faster. Continue to use your coping and self-care strategies as you work through the trauma.

Take some time to think about where you started after the trauma and how far you have come since then. It is easy to overlook progress, but it is important not to.

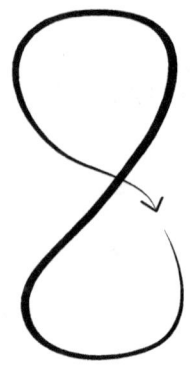

"It feels like the pain is never going to end."

The Pain Will Pass

In the midst of acute stress response or PTSD, it may feel like the pain will never end.

This is when it be helpful to talk to others who have had a similar experience-and survived. This can help you to have hope and believe that you, too, will survive the Valley.

As you gain some time and distance from the trauma, you may begin to notice that there are moments when you forget about it entirely for short periods of time. This is good. It means you are starting to reclaim your life.

It may be difficult to believe, but the time will come when the trauma will be part of your past, and not a constant demanding presence in your day-to-day life.

Hold onto this. You will make it through.

"I can't do this. It hurts too much."

If the Pain Feels Unbearable…

There may be times when the intensity of your trauma symptoms will feel unbearable.

The first thing to do is to let your support network know.

The second thing you need to do is be open to accepting help.

If you are not functioning well in your daily life, if each day seems an ordeal, then talk to your physician to see if there are additional supports that can be put into place (e.g., physician's order for reduced work hours, medical interventions).

Charting the intensity of your symptoms on a scale of 0–10 several times throughout the day can help identify whether there are specific periods of the day that tend to be more difficult for you. Charting can also help you to recognize periods of relief in your day and provide you with the confidence that it will not always be like this. The pain will pass.

"It's ridiculous. I'm always on guard for possible threats. I never feel safe anymore."

Establishing Safety

Following trauma, one's sense of safety in the world is undermined. Things like this do not usually happen to people, but they *actually happened to you*.

For a time after the trauma, you may notice that you are much more alert to possible threats in your environment. You may even begin consciously to change some of your behaviours to try to minimize these threats.

It is important to re-establish a sense of safety in your world. This may involve taking steps to ensure your home is more secure so you can begin to allow your body to relax again (e.g., upgrade locks, install an alarm system).

This may also involve finding people with whom you feel safe to talk about your trauma, subsequent fears, and need to feel secure.

Noticing how your sense of safety has been affected and taking steps to re-establish it are essential for healing.

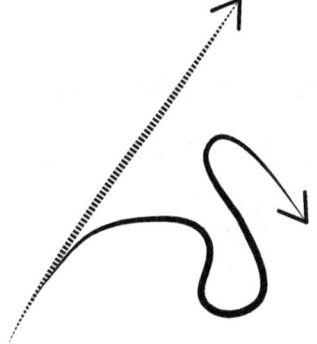

"There are times when I don't trust myself."

Develop a Safety Plan

If you are prone to suicidal thoughts or self-harming behaviour, it would be wise to develop a safety plan.

It is best to work on this plan before you need it. List everything you can think of that helps you to deal with stress, or that can calm, comfort, and distract you when you are feeling overwhelmed.

Here are some examples of the types of things that people include in their safety plans:

- call a friend
- watch a movie
- work out at the gym
- take a hot bath
- listen to favourite music

Once you make your safety plan, keep it in a place where it will be easy to find when you need it. You can continue to add ideas to your list over time.

"I want to crawl into bed and curl up in a ball, so I can escape life."

Create a Self-Care Box

For the times when you are in the darkness and cannot remember what light looks like, having a self-care box can help.

Prior to your next dark time, fill a box (the size of a shoe box) with things that will remind you of what is good in your life - maybe pictures of your partner, children, dog, friends, or favourite vacation spots. Add letters, poems, quotes, and pieces of art and music that encourage you.

Next, add some distractions-art supplies, a good book you have wanted to read, a puzzle, a crossword book.

Then, add some objects to help you stay in the moment by using some or all of your senses (e.g., candy, a favourite tea, a shell, fragranced essential oil).

Decorate your box, if you like, and place it somewhere obvious so that you will remember it is there and be able to get to it when you are having a difficult time.

"There is something about nighttime that makes it the worst part of my day."

Nighttime Is Often the Hardest

Maybe it is because of the natural vulnerability of sleeping that many people find nighttime the hardest. The window between 2:00 a.m. and 5:00 a.m. seems particularly difficult.

Insomnia. Night waking. Nightmares. Night terrors. These can make the dark hours seem endless.

Rational thought often departs during the darkest hours of the night. Fear curls up in its place, making it difficult to relax. Shadows and sounds that you do not even notice in the daylight, may become threatening and foreboding.

If nighttime is hardest for you, think about what you might do to blunt its effects. Would using a night light help? How about playing soft music or installing a lock on your bedroom door? Would it help to write yourself a calming letter that you could read at these times? What else might help increase your sense of safety and peace at night?

"I'm thinking of moving to another city, just to get away from this place."

This Isn't the Time for Major Decisions

Now is not the time to make major life decisions unless they are absolutely necessary.

Your body and mind are under enough stress already. In this state, you are unlikely to see or be able to process the full picture. Under less stress, your perception may be entirely different.

If you can, hold off for a while on making major decisions regarding:

- a relationship (i.e., starting or ending one - unless it's an abusive relationship that you must leave for safety reasons)
- work
- finances
- relocation

Waiting until you are in a more stable, relaxed physical and emotional state will help you to make better decisions.

"I just need some time alone."

Cocooning for Awhile is Okay

There may be times when you need to withdraw from the busyness of life for awhile. To quiet yourself. To rest. To gather your energy.

Cocooning can be a helpful healing strategy.

Some people need to take time from work or school. Others are able to continue functioning in these areas but decide to scale back social functions.

Cocooning needs are individual.

You will know when and how to cocoon.

Trust yourself to know what you need, and give yourself permission to take some time for this important activity.

"Crying makes me feel weak."

It's Okay to Cry

In the aftermath of trauma, you can experience several very intensely felt emotions. Sadness, hurt, frustration, anger, and disappointment may be some of them.

It is okay to cry. Sometimes people are afraid to cry, thinking that if they start they will never stop. Rest assured: that will not happen. Crying has a beginning, a middle, and an end.

Crying cleanses emotional wounds just as blood cleanses a physical wound.

Crying is not a sign of weakness. It is a sign of healthy, normal, emotional functioning.

After a good cry you may be exhausted and need to sleep. That is okay and quite natural. A good emotional cleansing can be exhausting.

"I like to write, because then what I'm feeling is outside of me where I can look at it, rather than inside tearing me apart."

Get It Out

Emotions have a physiological component. Prolonged stress can take a toll on your body.

Although it is important to acknowledge your emotions and work at decreasing distress, it can also be helpful to find ways to express negative emotions so that they are represented outside of your body. This is called *externalizing*.

Moving the negative emotions from inside your body, where they can cause destruction, to a neutral or positive position outside, typically involves some form of creative or physical action. Methods commonly used include:

- writing
- playing an instrument
- photography
- drawing/painting or sculpting
- working out

Externalizing allows you to transform the potentially harmful energy of negative emotions into something meaningful and positive.

"How am I going to get through this?"

Find Your Motivation

When the climb gets difficult and you trip and fall, what strength will you draw on in order to get back up again? What will help to keep you moving during those moments when you feel you cannot take another step?

You need to identify your motivation.

For some people, motivation comes in the form of rage and the conviction that they have lost too much already. They are not willing to let the trauma take anything more away from them.

Some people are motivated by thoughts of their loved ones: their partners, friends, children, or grandchildren.

Some find their motivation in their desire to "win" against the trauma.

Still others find their motivation in their hopes and dreams for the future.

Whatever it is, motivation can be your secret weapon and an extraordinary tool during the hardest parts of the climb out of the Valley.

Find yours and keep it close to your heart and mind throughout the journey.

"I try to research on the Internet what's wrong with me and what I can do to get better but a lot of what I read just confuses and upsets me more."

The Internet: Friend or Foe?

The Internet can be a very valuable resource for information on many topics, including traumatic stress. There are many credible sites available to provide you with evidence-based information. Some survivors of trauma, however, find the abundance of information available online - especially the graphic personal stories - to be overwhelming.

If surfing the Internet for information is taking up a lot of your time and causing you more distress than comfort, you may wish to give it a break. During this part of your healing journey, the focus needs to be on gathering tools to reduce distress and increase stabilization. Bring your questions and concerns to your therapist, counsellor, or physician for discussion.

It is also important to remember that although traumatic stress presents itself in some common ways, each person will experience it individually. Your trauma story and the meanings it holds are unique to you. The pathways that other people have found to lead them out of the Valley may or may not be part of your journey.

"I am a person of faith and I cannot come to terms with the confusion I am feeling related to my faith in God and the horror of the trauma and its effects."

How Do Your Faith and Spirituality Fit into All of This?

The next three sections will have the most relevance for readers with a religious faith. The commentary contains thoughts that people of faith may find helpful and reassuring as they struggle with the impact trauma has had on their faith and spirituality. Your counsellor may or may not feel comfortable in providing assistance in this area. Whether or not he or she engages with you on these and other topics of spirituality, you may well find helpful guidance from your minister, priest, rabbi, imam or other spiritual leader.

"I haven't been able to pray since this happened."

Honest Prayer

Sometimes people of faith find it difficult to pray following a traumatic event. They may wonder where their God was during the event and why He or She did not do something to help.

If you felt abandoned or betrayed by your Higher Power during the traumatic experience, consider that He or She is already aware that you feel that way.

The most helpful and healing prayer is often an honest prayer. Tell God (while admitting it to yourself) how you are feeling and what you have been thinking. Although an omniscient God will already know all of this, you may need to come face to face with it yourself in order to come to a place of peace.

Honest prayer might be a means to reconnect you with your Higher Power and allow you to begin to integrate your faith with your experience.

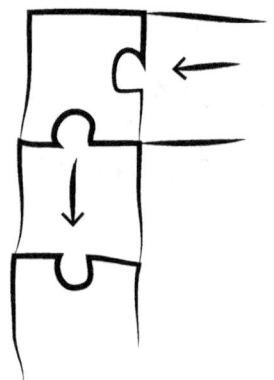

"Some people say this was part of God's plan. That's not the God I believe in."

Part of God's Plan?

It can be repugnant to think that trauma is part of God's plan for anyone. That kind of thinking can lead you to feel alienated from your Higher Power and your spirituality - at a time when you need them the most.

It might be more helpful to consider that God's plan for humankind in general involves laws of nature and free choice, as well as laws of cause and effect. With this understanding it is more likely that your experience of trauma occurred as a result of one or more of these universal principles.

Although your Higher Power may not have directly intervened during the trauma you experienced, that does not mean He or She was absent. Some people find comfort in their belief that during times like that God may have been weeping right alongside them while waiting for an opportunity through nature or other people to respond.

Your faith, and the inner strength it gives you, can offer you help through the hard times if you are open to it.

"I ask God for help but there doesn't seem to be any answer."

Recognizing Angels

Unlike the stories you may have read in sacred text, it is not often these days that we hear of God answering prayers via an otherworldly messenger or a burning bush.

As part of the gift of free will, it is up to individuals to decide whether to be an instrument for God's plans. It is likely, therefore, that the answers to your prayers and healing opportunities will come through your contact with other people.

The angels your Higher Power sends your way might not be easily recognized if you do not know what you are looking for.

It could be the stranger who smiles at you when you feel lonely, a friend who leaves a message to tell you that you are thought of, or the laughter of a child that touches your heart.

Try to be aware of these angels - you can recognize them by their just-in-time messages of hope, comfort, and love.

Reflections

1. What healthy coping strategies have you used to deal with distressing trauma-related symptoms? What *un*healthy coping strategies have you used?
2. What new coping strategies that you have read about in this book are you willing to try?
3. Is there anything in this Part of the book that you found comforting and that you would like to keep in mind during your journey out of the Valley. If so, what is it?

Use the space below to write down your reflections on these questions as well as others posed in the sections in this Part.

PART FOUR

HEALING AND FINDING YOUR PATHWAY OUT OF THE VALLEY

On the last part of the journey, individuals often accept or come to terms with what has happened to them. This is not to be confused with condoning it! You may revisit moments of the traumatic experience in therapy in order to help your body and mind recognize that the trauma is over and you have survived. This is where your mind and body relearn how to feel safe and relaxed again. During this part of the journey you might travel down paths related to grief, anxiety, rage, trust, guilt, and/or forgiveness. This takes courage. You can do it. You are strong and you are healing. You have the tools and strength to finish the climb. They are the pathways out of the Valley. They focus not only on the past and present, but on the future as well.

The insights and tools in this Part are meant to help you manage the steepest parts of the climb. They are meant to support you as you continue to heal and begin to integrate your history of trauma into who you are as a person. Integrating the trauma does not mean that you become defined by it, but rather that it is something that *happened to you* in the past. It is not who you *are*.

It is important to remember that healing is an individual journey with no specified timelines. Trust the quiet wisdom of your body and mind to find the paths and timelines that are right for you.

"I think I am ready to get on with this."

When Is It Time to Finish the Climb?

It is time to finish the climb out of the Valley when you:

- are no longer in crisis and have found tools that work to reduce distress to a tolerable level when it arises
- feel stronger
- are living in a safe environment
- have a good therapist and a few friends who will walk beside you through the final parts of the journey ahead
- can hear the wise "voice" of the warrior inside and he or she says it is time to climb out
- are aware of the needs of your body and mind and are willing to take breaks as required

"I don't want to tell people what happened. It makes me feel weak and ashamed. Do I have to tell them everything?"

Your Story Is Sacred

It may seem like an unlikely description of one of the worst experiences of your life, but it is true that your story is *sacred*.

Your story is as personal as it gets. It belongs to you. In the details of your story are your fears, strengths, doubts, resiliency, and vulnerabilities. This is why you are not obliged to share your story with everyone.

Choose your listeners carefully.

In telling your story, you are allowing another person access to a part of yourself that was wounded. Choose people who you know are trustworthy, nonjudgmental, supportive, and compassionate. If confidentiality is important to you, choose people who will respect it.

You have the right to choose what parts of your story to tell, and when and to whom you will tell them. This story belongs to you.

"It should have been me."

Survivor Guilt

Following a trauma in which others are seriously injured or killed, a sense of guilt among survivors can result.

The knowledge that it could just as easily have been you increases empathy with those who fared worse. You might wonder why you survived and someone else did not. You might even begin to try to compare the value of your life against the value of the lives of those more seriously impacted by the trauma.

This sort of thinking can lead down a guilt-inducing and destructive path.

To begin to heal, you need to remind yourself of some truths on a daily (and perhaps hourly) basis:

- the traumatic event is over
- you cannot change the past
- you survived and your life is waiting for you to heal, engage, and live

The guilt you feel for having survived is of no service to you or the world.

"I've lost so much."

Taking Stock of the Losses

With trauma, there are always significant losses.

You might experience more than one type of loss.

There may be physical or relational losses because of injury or death.

Losses may also be emotional, such as a lost sense of safety or trust.

Losses may be connected to a shattered belief system that you once held dear, such as a belief in a just or fair world.

Sometimes the biggest loss of all is the loss of potential-the loss of a dream for a particular future or the way you thought your life would unfold *but for the fact of the trauma*.

To begin to grieve losses and heal from them, you must first identify what they are.

"There are times when I think I will drown in my tears."

Grief

Grief is part of the healing process as you come to terms with your losses.

Grieving is neither a clean nor elegant step-by-step process, but rather a complex emotional, physical, and thought process that takes a lot of energy.

The emotions involved can get messy-with anger, sadness, guilt, despair, relief, and acceptance seemingly coming and going as they please.

At times it may feel as if you are moving in circles. That is because grief often involves healing in layers.

Remember that grief is part of the healing process and you will get through it.

There is no set timeline involved. It will take however long it takes. Be patient and know you are moving through it.

"I cry at work, at the shopping centre, anywhere and everywhere."

Scheduling Grieving

If your grief is coming out seemingly whenever it pleases throughout your day, and you are feeling overwhelmed by it, it is time to start to contain it.

Scheduled grieving works well for some people, but it takes practice and determination. It involves setting aside a time each day for grieving. A period of 30 or 40 minutes a day works for most people. So, if you decide that 7:30 p.m. is your time to grieve, you will set your alarm for either 30 or 40 minutes later. At 7:30 p.m. you can review your losses, allow yourself to cry, write, listen to music…do whatever you need to do to grieve. However, when your alarm sounds, you must stop. Wash your face. Get a drink of water. Move on to something else.

If your grief arises outside of your scheduled time, remind yourself that you will get to it at the allotted time but not outside of that time frame. Do not entertain it at other times. Distract yourself or concentrate on something else.

Your body and mind will learn that there is a time and a place for grief, and that you are not ignoring your grief but rather honouring it by making a time for it each day. Giving it a scheduled time means your grief no longer has to interrupt to try to get your attention throughout your day. It will be heard.

"I feel like damaged goods."

Injured-Not Damaged

After trauma some people come to believe that their value as a person has been irreparably damaged. When this happens it not only causes unnecessary grief and pain, but it also interferes with your ability to heal.

In such instances, a shift in self-perception is required. Considering yourself to have been *injured* or *wounded*, instead, may allow you to let go of the negative value judgments that can come with the term *damaged*. As human beings, we can heal from injuries and wounds.

As with all injuries and wounds, there will be scars, both seen and unseen. Regardless of your losses, it is critical that you understand that *your value remains intact*.

"I should have handled the situation better."

Practise Compassion

Following trauma it can be tempting to feed and grow thoughts and feelings related to blame and judgment.

If other people experienced the trauma with you, or responded to you following the trauma, you may be disappointed by how they reacted. Or, you may be disappointed by how you reacted.

Remember that everyone responds to traumatic situations differently than they would to ordinary events in life.

Compassion for others, and yourself, can help move your healing along.

Acknowledging feelings of disappointment, hurt, and anger is necessary for healing.

Consciously choosing not to dwell or obsess on thoughts and feelings related to blame and judgment is a healthy decision. Growing these monsters will serve only to poison your body, mind, and relationships.

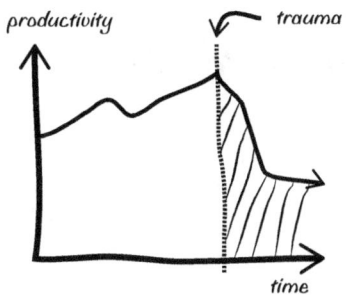

"Before this happened, I was much more productive. Now it seems I can barely keep up with my life."

Taking Your Circumstances into Account

When you are dealing with severe trauma reactions, it is unrealistic to expect yourself to function and perform as you would in "ideal" circumstances. Clearly, these are *not* ideal circumstances.

Just because your 100% effort may have seemed more productive when you were not dealing with trauma, it does not mean that you are somehow slacking off.

Dealing with trauma takes a tremendous amount of energy. It may well be that you are using the same energy as before but 70%–80% of it is consumed in coping.

Looking at it from this perspective, you may more accurately begin to see how incredibly adaptive you are.

"I don't understand why this happened."

It May Never Make Sense

It is normal to want to understand why such a devastating event occurred. However, the *why* questions of trauma are seldom answered in a satisfactory way.

If there were other people involved, you may want to understand what their motivations were.

In the end, regardless of whether you come to an understanding of why the trauma happened, it will not change the fact that it did happen.

Some people spend months, even years, trying to understand something that may never make sense to them. This can waste valuable time and energy that could be used for healing and living.

You have a life to live. Set limits around your need to understand *why*.

Accept that you may never fully understand why the trauma happened. This lack of understanding does not have to interfere with your healing journey. You can heal without having answers to the *why* questions.

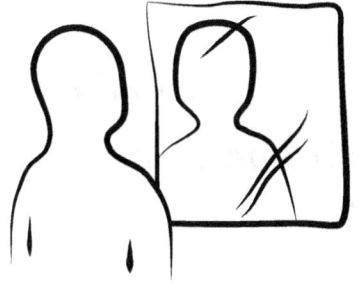

"I look back and am left with a ton of guilt and think that if only I had made different choices this wouldn't have happened."

Hindsight Is a Double-Edged Sword

In any situation, you are able, after the fact, to view things in a new light. Previously unknown consequences become obvious.

You have the opportunity to learn things of great value from what happened and its aftermath and to move forward in life equipped with these new experiences and knowledge.

Unfortunately, following trauma, people often use this new knowledge to beat themselves up with guilt over what they think they *could have* or *should have* done instead.

Taking into account the tremendous strain your body and mind were under during the trauma and the information you had at those moments, it is important to recognize that the decisions you made were likely the ones that made the most sense to you *at the time*. Acknowledge this. Let go of the guilt. You are human and did your best. It is now time to focus on healing.

"I feel this overwhelming sadness that never seems to leave."

Ongoing Depression

Depression is a physiological illness with emotional symptoms. Trauma can trigger depressive symptoms.

Here are some symptoms of depression that you may experience:

- fatigue
- concentration and memory difficulties
- feelings of hopelessness, despair, and/or guilt
- loss of interest in things you used to enjoy
- irritability and anger
- ongoing sadness
- changes in eating, weight, behaviours, and/or sleeping patterns
- thoughts of suicide

If the above symptoms persist beyond two weeks, speak with your doctor. *If the symptoms include suicidal thoughts and urges, contact your counsellor and your doctor **immediately**.*

"I'm constantly worried. It seems like it's my 'new normal.'"

Persistent Worry

During traumatic experiences your world and your beliefs can be turned upside down.

Afterwards your mind might be challenged in trying to integrate the traumatic experience into your belief system, while also coming to terms with your vulnerability.

Having experienced the sense of helplessness and horror that are part of trauma, you are recognizing how vulnerable you can be.

It can be a challenge to remind yourself that the danger is over and there are situations in which it is okay to relax and let down your guard. At first, this will likely have to be a conscious effort on your part.

Although, for a while, you may naturally imagine and search out potential threats in your environment, it will be important also to acknowledge safety in your environment.

Notice the safe people and places in your life. Consciously choose to let your guard down when you are physically and emotionally safe.

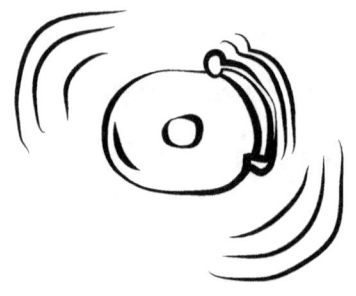

"I've started having panic attacks."

Ongoing Anxiety

Anxiety disorder is a physical illness with emotional components.

Common symptoms of anxiety that you might experience include:
- difficulty breathing
- fear
- feeling hot and/or sweating
- stomach pain
- nervousness
- shaking or trembling
- heart racing
- panic attacks

If the above symptoms persist beyond two weeks, speak to your doctor.

"I don't want to take medication."

The Question of Medication

Unfortunately, depression, anxiety, and related insomnia can be part of the traumatic stress reaction.

It is important to remember that your symptoms have a physiological basis. They are *not* the result of a character flaw or weak willpower.

There are times when it is appropriate for your physician to prescribe medication to help to alleviate serious symptoms. This can be especially important if you are so overwhelmed by your symptoms that you are unable to function in your daily activities.

Medication is often a temporary measure that will allow you to access more of your energy so that you can use it to develop coping strategies and focus on healing. Only you and your doctor can assess what is in your best interest.

"I feel so angry. Any little thing will set me off!"

Transforming Anger

Anger, even rage, is a normal response to trauma.

The energy of anger is physical and emotional. It resides in your body.

Where does your anger sit? If your anger resides in your legs, and you are physically able to, you may want to expend some of that energy in sports such as soccer, running, and kickboxing.

If the energy of anger resides in your arms, and you are able to, you might want to expend some of that energy in sports such as baseball, boxing, and tennis.

Working out with weights, while concentrating on releasing your anger as you expend energy, can be helpful, too.

The bottom line is to find ways to *transform* the potentially destructive energies of anger into strength and a sense of accomplishment.

"At first, trying to relax during a massage was a challenge. Now I fall asleep within minutes."

Therapeutic Massage

Therapeutic massage by a licensed professional can alleviate stress and muscle pain in your body. It can also help retrain your body to relax.

In choosing a massage therapist, it is important to find someone with whom you feel safe and comfortable.

You may want to try a few different massage therapists until you find one that you like.

Booking a massage at the end of your day, and following up with an Epsom salt bath, can help you feel sleepy and relaxed at bedtime.

"I want to find something good to take from this."

Finding Meaning or Purpose

For some people, it is important to find meaning or purpose following trauma. This might involve looking for a *silver lining* or trying to focus on the positives that came out of the trauma experience.

If you are a person for whom finding meaning or purpose is important, take the time to think about your trauma experience and talk to others who have been through a similar one.

Sometimes, finding meaning or purpose will involve volunteering or contributing to a cause connected to your trauma experience.

Sometimes it will involve sharing your story with others so that they, too, can learn from it and walk away with hope.

Sometimes it will involve helping others who have survived similar traumas.

And, sometimes it will involve focusing on gratitude for your inner strength and the supportive people who helped you get through.

"If only I had..."

Forgive Yourself If Need Be

None of us is perfect. As human beings, there are times when all of us make mistakes in behaviours and judgments.

Sometimes we have "gut feelings" that we choose to ignore. At other times, we have no warning at all that things are going to end up very badly.

If you made a mistake that caused harm to someone and you are carrying guilt, it may help to ask for forgiveness.

More often than not, however, the person from whom you need forgiveness most is yourself.

Not forgiving yourself will cause continued suffering for you and those who love you.

Not forgiving yourself will not change what happened.

If you want to truly heal, and are blaming yourself for what happened, one of your healing paths might involve learning how to forgive yourself.

"If I don't do things perfectly, I feel like I am not good enough."

Love Yourself-Shadow and Light

You do not need to be perfect in order to be *good enough*. You have always been good enough. Nothing will change that.

The challenge in healing and life is not to be perfect, but to be *perfectly you* - with all the *light* (i.e., strengths, joys, triumphs, and hopes) and *shadow* (i.e., weaknesses, disappointments, and frustrations) that define who you are.

The adventure is in consciously and continuously shaping who you are by your choices and attitudes.

In this world there is only one you. No one else has your set of experiences, qualities, knowledge, wisdom, and insights.

You have much to learn and to teach in this lifetime, in ways that are unique to you. The world needs you.

Choose to let go of the need to be someone other than the person you were meant to be. Love yourself - shadow and light.

 *"I want to forgive but don't know how."*

Choosing to Forgive Others

Sometimes trauma occurs because of the intentional or accidental behaviours of others. In these cases the question of forgiveness can be a difficult one to wrestle with.

For some people, it is not necessary to forgive to move forward with their healing. Others, however, feel stuck if they cannot forgive.

Forgiveness can be a way of freeing yourself from bitterness and resentment. It can be a healing gift to yourself.

Forgiveness is not about forgetting something that hurt you or pretending that it does not matter. On the contrary, it is about acknowledging that the injury is significant. It is also about acknowledging that there is nothing that the person who caused the trauma can do to make it right.

In the act of forgiveness, you accept that the debt can never be adequately repaid. With this acceptance and the letting go of blame, anger, and judgment, peace will often enter.

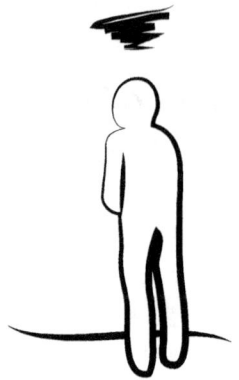

"I can't forgive this."

Choosing Not to Forgive

As mentioned previously, not everyone finds it desirable or necessary to forgive others in order to heal. That is your decision to make. The only caution to bring to your attention is that if the anger and bitterness towards another person starts to take over your life, then you might be someone who needs to forgive for your own wellbeing. (see Choosing to Forgive regarding why this might be helpful for you).

Then there are those who want to forgive, but find they are unable to at the present time because the trauma injury is so raw and painful. Adding guilt for not being able to forgive in the moment, adds to the burden of distress. For you it might make sense to let it be for now and focus on your healing. If forgiveness is important to you, the path will present itself at the appropriate time.

There are also situations in which it might be best not to forgive until you sort out what forgiveness means for you. If you have been taught that forgiveness requires you to forget what happened and act like it didn't happen, and you have been traumatized by someone in your life who continues to be abusive towards you, then forgiveness is not a healthy or safe choice right now because, according to this definition, it would place you (and possibly others) in ongoing danger. In this case, working on a definition of forgiveness that takes into account your need for safety would be important for your healing.

"For a week now I've been feeling sad and out of sorts and I'm not sure why."

Preparing for Anniversaries

When a trauma anniversary date approaches, you may notice a recurrence of your original trauma symptoms. Grief and sadness will often surface as well.

Even if you are not consciously aware of the date, your body remembers.

Remembering the trauma on anniversaries is part of the process of honouring what you lived through and letting go.

It is also an opportunity to reflect on how far you have come.

If you are concerned that your trauma anniversary might be difficult for you, it is important to plan. Keep your calendar clear of extra commitments. You may want to schedule time to reflect on the trauma and, in some special way, to honour your survival. Remind people who care about you of this upcoming date so that they can be mindful of it and ready to offer extra support if needed.

Different people respond to trauma anniversaries in different ways. Be a respectful witness to *your way*.

 *"What's wrong with me?"*

Asking More Adaptive Questions

When stressful situations arise, what kind of questions do you ask yourself? Are they adaptive and supportive?

Think about a moment recently when you were feeling overwhelmed. What questions did you ask yourself?

Consider how the following questions could affect your thinking, body, and emotions: "Why does this always happen to me? What if I mess up again?" Ask yourself these questions out loud. How do you feel emotionally? How does your body feel?

Next, try asking yourself (again aloud) these questions: "What is my priority for this moment? What do I need right now to get through this?" Notice how you feel. Notice how your body feels when you ask the questions. How do your feelings compare to how you felt when you asked the previous questions?

Our brain's job is to try to answer the questions we ask it. It does not judge whether our questions are slanted to be self-critical or encouraging.

How can you adjust the questions you ask yourself throughout your day to make your focus and answers more supportive?

 *"I'm my own worst critic."*

Improving Your Self-Talk

Most people are only vaguely aware of the types of things they say to themselves on a daily basis.

There is a script that plays in your thoughts throughout the day: a commentary on life, yourself, your experiences, and other people.

For the most part, this script was never intentionally written, but rather is a compilation of your observations from life experience, as well as what you may have learned from important people in your life.

Your script has a huge impact on your perceptions, feelings, and physical state.

If this script is negative and self-critical, it can be a source of tremendous emotional and physical distress.

Listening to your script, evaluating the supportiveness of the messages, and adjusting them where needed can have a major effect on how you feel about yourself and life.

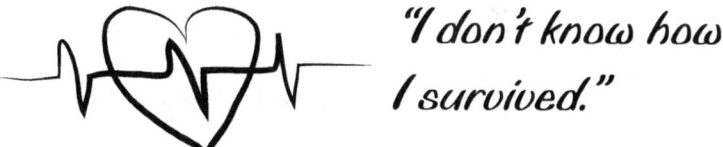

"I don't know how I survived."

Celebrate Your Survival

You are here today because you survived.

You may have suffered significant loss and injury, but you made it to today - and that fact is worth celebrating.

You are a testament to human strength and resiliency.

Your survival may well have been a miracle.

Taking time to grieve the losses is important - but so is taking time to celebrate your survival.

You made it. There are people in your life to whom that means the world. Celebrate with them.

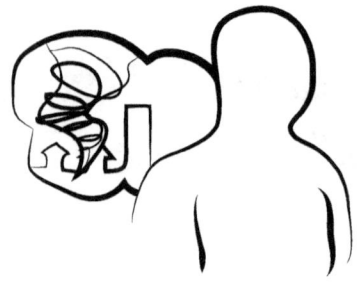

"I try to imagine a time when this is in my past - and not in my face every day."

Envision Your Future

Daydreaming about your future is an important way to reclaim your life.

The time will come when the trauma you experienced will be part of your history. It will be *that thing that happened in the past*. It will no longer intrude on your daily life.

Envisioning the details of your future helps to prepare your body and mind to move forward.

Focusing on the details of where you want to be in the future - seeing it, feeling it, hearing it in your daydreams - will give you a goal to work toward and strength in times of darkness.

Set aside some time each day to dream your healing and future into being.

"I don't want to become a bitter person."

Who Do You Want to Be?

In the aftermath of trauma, it is easy to forget who you are. The emotions or numbness can feel so overwhelming that you may think that you have lost yourself. You have not.

You are, however, at an important crossroads. You have some very important decisions to make about what kind of person you will be following your traumatic experience.

Trauma can change you for the worse if you allow it to do so. Given your losses, it is easy to be negative, resentful, and bitter. However, being that way will not help you to heal and will only prolong your suffering.

Alternatively, you can choose to be open to the positive, to healing, and even to gratitude.

The attitude you choose and decisions you make on a daily basis will shape your person and your future.

Imagine yourself five years from now. Where do you want to be on your path to healing? What kind of person do you want to be? What small steps can you take today to move yourself in these directions?

"There are certain people I just can't be around anymore."

Surround Yourself with Positive People

The attitudes of those around us can affect our thoughts, emotions, and behaviours.

Negative people can drain you of energy and hope. Their negativity can increase your stress level and influence your perceptions of yourself and the world around you.

You have been through enough, and your energy is limited. Where possible, limit your contact with negative people.

Invest your time and energy in people who add something positive to your life or perspective.

Hope, compassion, gratitude, and joy are invaluable gifts that people can give each other. Allow yourself to receive and give these gifts.

"I don't have time to do things for me."

Make Time for Things You Enjoy

Part of reclaiming your life is to ensure you have time for doing things that give you joy.

What activities have, in the past, made you feel glad to be alive?

What activities give you a sense of purpose and meaning?

What makes you smile and laugh? What makes you forget your challenges for a while?

You need to make time for these healthy activities again. It is time to reconnect with people.

It is time for you to laugh again, to dream again, and to live again.

It is time to find joy again.

"I find peace through walking in the woods."

Nature Can Be Healing

For some people, nature is healing. Walking in the forest, sitting by a lake, looking up at the stars, or listening to raindrops fall...some people find peace and inspiration in nature.

Experiencing the wonders of nature can also provide a larger perspective.

The vastness of nature and its grandeur can help you to see beyond the scope of your own challenges.

Have you ever noticed a tree growing in an improbable environment, such as in a crevice or on a rock? That is the persistent force of nature at work. In times of difficulty, you can take inspiration from that tree. You, too, can be determined to grow and heal despite the challenges that face you.

"I feel like people are looking at me and thinking that I'm broken."

You Are Not Your Trauma

Some people experience nagging doubts about their value as a person following trauma. They might believe that because of the experience they are somehow tainted, or not as good as other people. This is not true.

You have had to deal with extraordinary challenges and loss, but you have done it.

The trauma has stretched you beyond what you knew you were capable of.

You have demonstrated your resiliency and persistence in moving past it.

You are an incredible human being and have much to be proud of.

"I don't feel strong."

Acknowledge Your Strength

You may not feel like it, but the truth is that you are a strong person.

You are resilient.

You are adaptable.

You are a survivor.

Believe in yourself. Acknowledge the warrior inside.

You have already survived the impossible.

You are on your way out of the Valley.

 *"I feel different."*

You Have Changed

It is not a judgment or criticism - it is a fact that you have changed.

As a result of surviving trauma, you have been stretched beyond your limits and you have survived.

The *old you* has been integrated with the *new you*. You are a combination of both.

Each day of our lives we change as we learn and grow. Trauma accelerates that process.

You have experienced significant losses that have changed your life, at least for a time. Even after you heal and recover from your symptoms, the trauma will be part of your history. It will shape how you see yourself and your life.

Change is going to happen each day of your life. Although during the trauma you had no control over the direction your life took, now the control is yours. Change can happen in an instant, or slowly over time. You have some control over how you change and move forward from here.

How do you wish to proceed?

"I'm not sure where to go from here."

Today Is a New Day

Today stands before you as a new day. You can choose how you will use it.

The past is what it is. You cannot change it.

The exciting part about being an adult is that you get to choose where you go from here.

The only power the past has today is what you choose to give it. Your past does not have to be your future.

Today is filled with potential. What will you do with it?

The choice is yours to make.

"I'm starting to get my life back."

Time to Live Your Life

The time will come when you no longer think about your trauma first thing in the morning and last thing at night.

The time will come when you remember it as something awful that happened in the past but is over. It will no longer have the power to overwhelm you or cause you emotional and physical distress.

It will be part of your history.

You will start to live more often in the present than in the past.

If this is happening for you, it is time to celebrate! Call your loved ones and plan a party.

You are well into the process of reclaiming your life.

"I feel like I've come a long way, but some days are still a challenge."

Life Is an Ongoing Journey

Finding your way out of the Valley does not mean that your life journey from here on will be problem free. There will still be unexpected bumps in the road that you will have to handle.

The good news is that surviving the Valley has left you much more skilled at coping with life's challenges, and it is to be hoped, more aware of your strength, adaptability, and resilience.

Reflecting on what you have been through and how far you have come in your healing can provide you with a new perspective and confidence in dealing with obstacles.

Life is an on-going journey. To some extent, the terrain ahead is unknown. However, you now know what you are capable of and who your supports are, and that can mean a world of difference.

Reflections

1. This is one of the steepest parts of the journey. What do you find most challenging about it? What do you need at this moment to help support you?
2. When you view yourself through the eyes of compassion, what do you see?
3. What encouraging words might you say to a friend who is going through a journey similar to yours?
4. When you dream about your future, one in which trauma is not your first thought in the morning and your last thought at night, what does that future look like?
5. How will you continue to honour and celebrate all that you have survived and accomplished on your journey?

Use the space below to write down your reflections on these questions as well as others posed in the sections in this Part.

APPENDIX

Additional Resources for Survivors of Trauma

*If you are still in crisis or easily triggered, you should not read the books marked with an asterisk until you are stabilized and have good distress reduction strategies because they contain some graphic descriptions of trauma that might be overwhelming and/or triggering.

For a General Understanding of Trauma

*Herman, Judith. 1997. *Trauma and recovery: The aftermath of violence – from domestic abuse to political terror.* New York: Basic Books.

*Rothschild, Babette. 2000. *The body remembers: The psychophysiology of trauma and trauma treatment.* New York: W.W. Norton.

Rothschild, Babette. 2011. *Trauma essentials.* New York: W.W. Norton.

For More Information about Therapies Used for PTSD

Bisson, Jonathan I., Roberts, Neil P., Andrew, Martin, Cooper, Rosalind & Lewis, Catrin. 2013. Psychological therapies for chronic post-traumatic stress disorder (PTSD) in adults. The Cochrane Library online: http://onlinelibrary.wiley.com/doi/10.1002/14651858.CD003388.pub4/abstract

For Increasing Distress Tolerance Skills

McKay, Matthew, Wood, Jeffrey C., & Brantley, Jeffrey. 2007. *The dialectical behavior therapy skills workbook: Practical DBT exercises for learning mindfulness, interpersonal effectiveness, emotion regulation & distress tolerance.* Oakland, CA: New Harbinger Publications.

For Survivors of Sexual Abuse

*Bass, Ellen, & Davis, Laura. 2008. The courage to heal (4th ed.): *A guide for women survivors of child sexual abuse 20th anniversary edition.* New York: Harper Collins.

For Those Struggling with Finding Meaning

Kushner, Harold S. (2004). *When bad things happen to good people.* New York: Anchor Books.

For Those Struggling with the Loss of a Loved One

Colgrove, Melba, Bloomfield, Harold H., & McWilliams, Peter. 1993. *How to survive the loss of a love.* Los Angeles, CA: Prelude Press.

For Veterans

*Grossman, Dave, Lt. Col. (2009). *On killing: The psychological cost of learning to kill in war and society.* New York: Little, Brown and Company.

www.ingramcontent.com/pod-product-compliance
Lightning Source LLC
Chambersburg PA
CBHW070620300426
44113CB00010B/1603